The Lamp and the Lullaby

The Lamp and the Lullaby

Tales from a Rural Childhood

BILL LONG

NEW
ISLAND

THE LAMP AND THE LULLABY
First published 2010
by New Island
2 Brookside
Dundrum Road
Dublin 14

www.newisland.ie

ISBN 978-1-84840-072-6

British Library Cataloguing Data. A CIP catalogue record for this book is
available from the British Library.

Book design by Inka Hagen

Printed in the UK by CPI Mackays, Chatham ME5 8TD.

New Island received financial assistance from
The Arts Council (An Comhairle Ealaíon), Dublin, Ireland.

10 9 8 7 6 5 4 3 2 1

To the memory of my grandfather,
Mickey 'The Caffler':
my mentor, my best friend and the greatest
influence on my life.

Also to the memory of
Aeronwy Thomas and Gilbert Bennett.

And for my grandchildren,
John, Laura, Sian, Riona, Donal, Gabrielle,
Aisling, Niamh, that they may have some inkling of
what life was like in another time, another place.

'Like Dolmens round my
childhood, the old people.'

John Montague

'Fight your little fight, my boy,
fight and be a man.
Don't be a good little, good little boy
Being as good as you can.'

'Don'ts', D. H. Lawrence

'There is always one moment in childhood
when the door opens and lets the future in.'

The Power and the Glory , Graham Greene

Introduction

The genesis of something is always of interest and sometimes of importance. *The Lamp and The Lullaby* began with a Father's Day gift to me, from my daughter. A gift of Frank McCourt's *Angela's Ashes*. She was astounded to find that I hadn't read the book and determined to right that lamentable lack. She exacted from me a promise to read it.

Before starting to read *Angela's Ashes*, I read the 'blurbs', or 'puffs', on the back cover. There was a quote from the author: 'My childhood was, of course, a miserable childhood. The happy childhood is hardly worth your while. Worse than the ordinary miserable childhood is the miserable Irish childhood, and worse yet is the miserable Irish Catholic childhood.' I was shocked by the arrogance of his statement – 'The happy childhood is hardly worth your while.' And his presumption that, in his scale of misery, 'worse yet is the miserable Catholic childhood' was beyond belief. I felt, instantly, impelled to reply; but, in fairness, I must first read the book. I had promised my daughter.

Reading the book, I was full of sympathy for, and empathy with, the children who suffered such deprivation. However there is much in it to offend any honest reader: the excessive anti-Catholic bias, so many attempts at poetic writing, resulting in purple passages that didn't quite come off. Fortunately for Frank McCourt the book did appeal to millions of people, in many countries. It just didn't work for me.

I decided that my best reply would be to tell my own story; the story of a happy, albeit impe-cunious, Irish Catholic childhood. Tales of a simple rural life; the kind of life G. K. Chesterton wrote of when he coined that memorable, oh so apposite, oxymoron – 'tremendous trifles'.

The kind of trifles you cannot marshal in the form of a diary or arrange in chronological order, in serried ranks, like soldiers on parade. I found it best, most natural, every time I sat down to write, just to open my mind and let the trifles, the stories, spill or creep onto the page of their own volition. Sometimes they spilled, boister-ously, claiming their place; other times they crept out inconspicuously, almost apologetically, from the cracks and crevices of memory, to stake a quiet claim. If a memory of something that happened when I was seven presents itself to me before something that happened when I was five, am I to say to it, 'You come too soon, go back and wait your turn!' Certainly not; that would be churlish, losing all spontaneity and naturalness. Born and reared in the country, as I was, I have that inbred dislike of the 'battery-reared' and must always opt for the 'free range'. So, from the 'free range' of my memory, for what they are worth, come these tremendous trifles, these tales from my rural childhood.

I remember something John Steinbeck said to me, when I met him at Sag Harbour in 1962, the year he published *Travels with Charley*, the memoir of his journey through America with his French Poodle, Charley. He held that truth for the writer, in writing a memoir, was not remembering literally what had happened. It was much more complex, more exacting, and exciting, than that. There were three elements involved: what *had* happened, what we would *like* to think might have happened and *how* we remembered it. There was, he said, a point where all three ele-ments came felicitously together, and that was the real truth. Sometimes then, he said, the writer, with integrity, patience and good luck, would find this point. I hope I have.

In writing my own story I was also cognisant of the advice given by Paul Gallico at a lecture of his which I attended in Colombia University forty years ago: 'The world was never changed by young men who flew to the moon, or risked their necks to write a piece about their sensations. But, sometimes, if one could have a worthwhile thought, hold it and polish it, and write it down where people could read it, one might move this tortured old planet an infinitesimal fraction in the right direction.' Indeed. Isn't that what striving to write well is all about; any serious writer's constant search for *le mot juste*; the desire to nudge this obdurate old world that smidgin in the right direction.

And that, in the end, is what Frank McCourt and I have attempted to do, each in his different way, and each writing about very different childhoods. His no more no less valid than mine for being miserable; mine, despite his denigration of happiness, no more no less valid than his for being happy.

Bill Long,
Dublin,
January 2010.

So on a sunny, wind-blown late-April afternoon, I came kicking and mewling into this world, aided by the ministrations of a rural midwife, under the watchful, unblinking gaze of the statue of the Virgin Mother.

I was born and grew up in an old thatched long-house on the Waterford Coast. It stood between two great lighthouses: Hook Head to the east and Mine Head to the south west. Hook Head, the oldest lighthouse in these islands, was not visible to us. It stood away behind Newtown Head and Brownstown Head. But with relentless regularity, at twenty-five-second intervals, its powerful shaft of light raked the night sky. Mine Head, the highest light on the Irish coast, was visible across a wide expanse of open, capricious water that whispered or boomed as wind and tide dictated.

Anchored way off south west of Hook Head was the Coningbeg Lightship. When fog surreptitiously crept in like massive rolls of white wool bandaging the adamantine cliffs of our black coast, then at twenty-second intervals the diaphonic fog signal on Coningbeg roared its warning to ships; a deep, reverberating boom, like the bellow of a wounded bull. So from my country cradle, lighthouse beam and boom were my lamp and my lullaby.

Our house stood at the seaward end of a deep, broad glen that ran two miles from twin hills, which we called mountains, to the sea. Small, fertile fields sloped down on both sides of the glen to a fast-flowing stream. At the crossroads behind our house, three narrow, white dirt tracks led off: one down to the sea, a second up the centre of the glen parallel with the stream to join the main Tramore–Dungarvan road and a third over the steep shoulder of Cheasty's Hill to The Uplands, the village and the school.

The long-house had been built by my maternal great-grandfather over a century before I was born. He built the adobe walls three feet thick to withstand the gales from the south west and the scudding rain off the sea. However, after a few winters he found that the thickness of the walls was of itself no proof against the damp. He then created his own method of damp-proofing.

Twice a year he mixed two parts cement with three parts whitewash and applied three coats to the outer walls and one coat to the inner walls. As damp-proofing went over a hundred years ago, that was adequate.

When the old man died and his son, my grandfather, took over the place, he decided in his greater wisdom that if he continued to apply two coats of whitewash every year, he would end up with walls five feet thick. Therefore, being a man of both sense and sensibility, he applied this 'special' wash only on 'special' occasions. For Stations Mass in May, at irregular intervals when one of the family visited from the USA, when there was a wake, a wedding or a birth – then the wash was applied.

With my grandfather's idiosyncratic imagination, he decided to use a different colour every time: pink, duck-egg blue, sky blue, dark blue, light green, dark green, primrose yellow, yellow ochre, white and cream. Or when the mischievous spirit moved him, he would mix some remarkable unnamed and unnameable colours from leftover tins stacked in the back of his 'workshop' (a lean-to shed built against the end wall of the cow-byre). My mother told me that no matter what colour he used, it was always referred to as *white*wash. She said that on the occasion of my birth, she was allowed to select the colour of the wash; this was the first time anyone had been allowed such privilege. She selected a pale blue, the same colour as the cloak on the statue of the Virgin Mary standing on the deep window ledge in her bedroom. The old man was delighted by that, saying, enthusiastically, 'A great choice, Margaret! A great choice! Pale blue *white*wash it'll be!' So on a sunny, wind-blown, late-April evening, three days after the wash had been applied, I came kicking and mewling into the world, aided by the ministrations of a rural midwife, and under the watchful, unblinking gaze of the Virgin Mother.

A year and a half later, under the same watchful gaze but in the tremendous heat of mid July, my only sibling, a brother, Michael, was born. I am told that, unlike me, he came very quietly into the world in the same room, under the protection of the same statue of the Virgin Mary. We grew up together, sharing everything, as close as two brothers so close in age can be.

These then are the first lovely things
— the first 'tremendous trifles' — of
which I have total recall. All related to
The Meadowstone, which still holds for
me, at seventy-eight, all the magic it
held for me so long ago when
I was just four years old.

At the end of our front yard, just beyond the gable of the house, the stream rushed by with a gentle, gurgling sound in spring and summer and a great rumbling rush in autumn and winter. It cascaded over the multicoloured abraded stones, now clear, now flecked with foam, depending on the season. On the other side of that stream was a little meadow and that meadow, just a few yards from the water's edge, is home to the first memory of which I have total recall, 'The Meadowstone'.

The Meadowstone was a large, flat piece of granite, about seven feet by four feet. It stood proud of the meadow grass by only six inches. I remember its lovely surface of yellow-green lichen. I remember how soft it was to the touch of my tiny fingers. Every fine day I was carried across the stream and placed on the big granite stone to play. My father had constructed a fence made of wattles all round the stone to prevent me from waddling away across the meadow. I had just begun to walk and, given free rein, I saw no reason to stop walking for as long as my legs held out. Michael, not yet walking, would be placed on the stone beside me. The Meadowstone, my grandfather told me, was placed there by druids a long time ago. A tribe of fairies, the Meadowstone Fairies, lived underneath the stone. He warned me that I must never do anything to annoy or disturb them. They only came out at night and did not like to be bothered by or indeed even seen by humans. He told some scary, if salutary, tales of what had happened to people who had seen the little people in the past. However, sitting on the soft, golden-green lichen-covered stone, neither my grandfather nor the fairies need have worried. I was more interested in the animal visitors who came to look at me than I was in the fairies.

Our two cows came and thrust their enormous heads in close to me and I could smell their hot, sweet, milky breath. I will always remember their big, soft, luminous, searching eyes; benevolent eyes that always promised something wonderful. I remember telling my grandfather in my halting, limited vocabulary that the cows were trying to look inside me. He laughed out loud at that and said, 'I wonder what they might see, Liam! I wonder what they might see!' Even at that early age I wanted to have names for everything. With some help from my mother I named the cows Sam and Sadie. Michael would just sit and gape at the cows, stabbing a tiny finger in the air and shouting, 'Moo! Moo!'

Another visitor was the old white donkey, Paycock, one of the great, great friends of my childhood. He would come and lean his old head over the wattle fence and stare at me for a long time. He looked so lovely, woolly, clean and sleepy that I always reached up to rub his wet nose. He would take this as an invitation to lick my hand. With a great 'hee-haw', he would stick out his long, pink tongue and proceed to lick my small hand with great gusto. At the first few licks I laughed, for they tickled me, but then the licks began to hurt and I cried out, 'Paycock! Paycock! Bold! Bold! Away! Away!' Someone would come running from the house and chase the poor old fellow away. Michael would babble and point after the departing donkey, screaming, 'Hoosh! Hoosh!' When poor Paycock had gone I would sit and cry for his return.

I think Paycock must have been forlorn too, for I could hear his loud 'Hee-haw! Hee-haw!' from the far end of the meadow. After much 'hee-hawing' from him and much calling 'Paycock!' from me, he would return slowly, his old head hanging low as if to say 'I'm sorry!' Then the little ritual of reconciliation would begin. I would hold out my hand and the old donkey would lick it with all the gentleness he could manage, looking at me with big, sad eyes. From that old donkey I had my first and best lesson in reconciliation, in the joy of mutual regret and caring and love. Strange as it may seem, I have learned as much, if not more, about love and loyalty from animals as I have from humans in a long, eventful and happy life.

The two dogs, Fin and Butcher, came every day to the Meadowstone and managed to wriggle through the wattle fence. They would lie in the sun, sleeping, snoring, sighing and farting. I would complain to my mother about 'the bad smell Butcher makes!' Still, despite the smell, Michael and I would find it so comforting to lie between the sleeping, snoring, farting dogs, using them as fine, soft, warm pillows on which we fell asleep. I would dream of the wonderful world of the fairies my grandfather had told me about. The different tribes, the Meadowstone fairies, the Mountain fairies from the twin hills that we called mountains at the top of our glen, the River fairies who lived along the riverbank and the Sea fairies who lived in the old disused lighthouse on the little offshore island below our house. Those Sea fairies were the most savage of all, my grand-father said, and were forever attacking the other tribes. I would often wake from my dreams with the shrill sounds of fairy battle ringing in my ears, unable for the moment to help the good fairies repel the bad.

Then I would lie beside the sleeping Michael and between the sleeping dogs, listening to the stream gurgling by, all my lovely warring fairies gone. For of course you never saw the fairies during the day, except in dreams. And I'd had my dreams for one day. Other adventures were calling and I must wait until tomorrow to revisit my 'glimpses of the moon'. Very often on moonlit nights I would get out of my bed and press my face against the ice-cold glass of the window. From there I could see the Meadow-stone very clearly. Sometimes I thought I saw, though I could never be certain, small people dancing on the Meadowstone.

Then once, just once, on a soft, moonlit summer night, I stole outside. Though fearful of crossing the stream, I did eventually cross it. I waited beside the stone, but there was no one there. After a while the moonlight that had been soft and warm and welcoming, full of the promise of fairies and adventure, seemed cold and menacing. I became afraid to cross back over the stream. I sat on the cold, dew-covered grass and cried. Then, in the great silence that surrounded me, I bellowed out as loudly as I could, 'Grandad! Grandad! Grandad!' and waited for an answer. There wasn't a sound. So I repeated my call. This time from the far end of the meadow came a loud 'Hee-haw! Hee-haw!' from Paycock. I stopped crying, reassured by the friendly call of the old donkey. Soon I could hear him plodding and 'hee-hawing' through the thick, dew-covered grass toward me. He stopped right in front of me, his fetlocks dripping dew, and, bending down, licked my face with his rough tongue. I spluttered and squinted under the rough, warm welcome. Then I stood up and put my arms round his neck and hugged him. That is how my grandfather found us when he came from the house in answer to my cries.

Every dry morning my mother would come with a large kish-full of newly washed clothes and spread them out to dry on the grass around the Meadowstone. When the wind was fresh she would use some stones taken from the stream to place on the edges of the various items, holding them in place. The great white sheets would billow when the wind got underneath them, making a lovely fluttering sound, a sound also heard when my grandfather took me fishing in his little sailboat. When he unfurled his mainsail it fluttered and billowed in the breeze, just like my mother's washing on the grass of our meadow. Smaller items of washing would work free of their 'moorings' and be blown across the meadow to anchor on the whins along the stream. After that I would sit very contentedly on the Meadowstone listening to the flapping of the sheets and watching the multicoloured small 'flags' flying in the breeze. I could imagine myself, my two dogs and Paycock in my boat at sea, sailing anywhere I wanted to sail. I was happy there at the centre of my own small wonderful world, contemplating the many tremendous trifles around me.

At seventy-seven, the Meadowstone still holds for me all the magic it held for me all those years ago when I was a small boy of four. It doesn't matter now that it wasn't put there by fairies a century ago, as my grandfather said, but rather by county-council workers when they widened the stream just a decade before I was born. It still remains a magical place, in the blessed country of my imagination, where I may wander as I please and be a child again. It will always be my wonderful country of standing still, where nothing has changed in all the changing years; an inviolable kingdom of memory and imagination.

3

About that time my father took us to the August Races in Tramore. For the first time we saw the 'furniture' of a racecourse. Wildly excited at what we saw, we were resolved to start improving 'our racecourse' right away.

Michael and I would play for hours on end along the bank of the stream. Ever since my father had taken us to see the Annual Regatta in Tramore Bay we had become fascinated by the boats. My father, who had a genius for making things of wood, made us a whole fleet of toy boats with sails of differing colours. Together Michael and I constructed a harbour of mud and small stones for these boats. Here they could ride at their little anchors out of the run of the stream. We regularly had regattas of our own with as many as twelve boats, each with its own name emblazoned on bow and stern. I remember how we laboured over these names, *Skylark*, *Curlew*, *Sea Princes* and a dozen others, all but forgotten now in the passing of the years. Just recently I found the eighteen-inch hull of the *Curlew* in a box in my attic, dismasted, her red sail faded grey and unfurled, lying on the deck, awaiting a favourable wind, her sailing days no more. Later, Michael and I were to construct another game which was to preoccupy us both well into our teens.

This game we created entirely from our own imaginations. It was a horse-racing game. I was about six years old at the time and Michael was four and a half. It all began with us looking through the only newspaper we got, the *Cork Examiner*. The sports pages always had wonderful photographs of racehorses: horses in many different modes, running, standing, jumping fences. One day, without thinking, Michael began cutting out the horses from the newspaper – the horses and the jockeys. They were of course limp; nevertheless, we would get our dice and place two cut-outs at one end of the big kitchen table. We would then throw dice to see whose horse came first to the other end. We would draw little lines in chalk along the edge of the table. Each throw of the dice would determine how many lines we moved our horses. But it was always sad for us to see the horses and jockeys in full flight lying limp on the table.

One day my father, looking at us play, asked us why we didn't get the horses to stand up. We explained how we just used the horses as we cut them from the paper. He suggested we get some stiff cardboard, stick the horse cut-outs to that, do another cut-out and then our horses would stand up. To keep them standing up he could make us a little wooden stand for each one. Our 'game' began to become a reality.

About that time my father took us to the August Races in Tramore. For the first time we saw the 'furniture' of a racecourse. Wildly excited at what we saw, we were resolved to get to work on improving 'our racecourse'. There was more to it than horses, with jockeys crouched on their backs, running between white railings. There was the grandstand, the weigh rooms, the winner's enclosure and the big notice board with the jockeys' names and their horses' numbers. And there was the parade ring and race cards. We came home from the races that evening, our minds a fever of excitement. It was difficult to sleep that night. We kept whispering across to each other from our little beds. Sharing thoughts of how to make our racing game look like the real thing. Eventually we fell asleep, promising each other that we would start work the next day.

Over the next six months Michael and I worked very assiduously at making our primitive game into a real racecourse. Grandfather found us a lovely piece of lightweight board, about five feet by three foot, among the many 'treasures' in the shed where he kept his paint tins. We needed more time now than mother could give us at the kitchen table, so the new base for our game was set on two milk churns in a quiet corner of the big kitchen. Here we worked and played at our game for a couple of hours every evening. At the end of many months' endeavour, and with help from my father and grandfather, we had all the necessary racecourse 'furniture' in place. We then decided that we should have a racing newspaper every week. Michael was the researcher and reporter, and I wrote all the copy for the paper. We published stories of trainers and jockeys and horses, as well as giving the programmes for at least two race meetings every week. For a little while we worked with the actual names of trainers and jockeys and horses, exactly as they were in the daily sports page of the *Cork Examiner*. But that didn't satisfy our desire to be original. We devised fictitious names for horses, trainers, owners and jockeys. This meant finding names for about thirty jockeys, twenty-five trainers and twenty owners. The only names we retained from the newspaper were those of the race-courses. To this day, I can remember only one of those names: the name of one of our top jockeys, E. E. English. I know that buried in an old cardboard box somewhere in my attic are the yellowing 'race cards' from that golden time. They would reveal many more names, but I am very reluctant to look for them. It might, I feel, in some way spoil the memory.

Michael and I derived so much pleasure from playing this racing game. We really became addicted to it. He more than I. He carried this love of horse racing into adult life and derived great enjoyment from it, travelling whenever he could to race meetings. For myself, I continued to be interested in the sport of kings but rarely attended any race meetings over the years. I do love to watch horse racing on television; the crowds, the horses, the vivid colours of the jockeys' silks, the close finishes, the incredible falls in the jump races. I just love that spectacle but have never been tempted to bet on the horses. I always feel that to do so would be to diminish, maybe even destroy, the great joy I get from just watching. And I never watch without thinking of two small boys playing their racing game on an old board spread across two milk churns on a flag floor in the corner of a country kitchen in another time, another place.

My father had a great talent for working with wood. This was never more evident than at Christmas. For all the childhood years when I believed in Santa Claus, I really thought that Santa must be a carpenter. Christmas after Christmas, my brother and I received the most wonderful presents from him, all made of wood. There were all kinds of wood, all with lovely delicate touches of coloured paintwork: motor cars, lorries, tractors, boats, sometimes fitted with clockwork movements. Occasionally someone outside the family kindly brought us a noisy present of a toy car or lorry made of tin with garish colours. At the time, I remember saying that they were not as good as Santa's lovely wooden toys.

Of all the wooden toys we received at Christmas, one stands out in my mind as being the most wonderful of all. It was a model of Tramore Racecourse: the course itself, with its miles of white railings, the ring, the paddock, the small stables, the weigh room, the clubhouse and grandstand. It was all done in the most beautiful wood of different shades, with the most discreet touches of paint. I can remember asking that particular Christmas morning how long it must have taken to make all this. And my father answered, 'A long time, Liam, a long, long time!' I also wondered, though I did not ask, how Santa knew Tramore Racecourse so well.

There are other memories of Christmas that will always remain. The Glen covered in snow and icy roads when we were able to skate our way to Mass on Christmas morning. We children that is. My grandfather and grandmother had to go in the little trap with old Paycock's hooves well covered in sacking to keep him from slipping. Mother and father walked, very gingerly, on the ice. Then the Mass itself, with the organ and all the special singing, and myself, resplendent in freshly starched white surplice. I remember Fr Jim saying he would not keep us long on such a cold morning. He had only one thing to say to us,

'Be kind to each other and be generous to those who have less than you have. And always remember to be like "The Humble Nazarene", who spent his first few hours in a draughty old stable.' On the evening of Christmas Day we always had rosary and benediction in the church. Late in the evening, dark would be coming on and dozens of candles were lit on the altar. The odour of the candlewicks and the smell of oil from the kerosene lamps combined to fill the church with a heady odour.

The organ music and the choir singing Christmas carols would make you feel as if you were halfway to heaven. Oh, yes, the memories of those wonderful 'wooden' Christmases will last forever!

4

Perhaps it is a throwback to those early years that to this day my favourite scent is the scent of roses. It needs only the sight of a rose or the scent of a rose to spark the memory of that multicoloured carpet of 'living' roses spread across the floor of our front yard on 'whitewashing day'. I can never pass a street-vendor selling roses without buying some, whether it be in Cork or in New York.

Among our neighbours in The Glen, our house was referred to in kindly jest as 'having more skins than an onion' and 'more colours than the rainbow'. My grandfather was always pleased, always glad, but never proud, as pride was something he did not countenance, that his house stood out in its many-coloured splendour against the green of the fields and the ever-changing colour of the sea. This many-coloured splendour was greatly added to from April to September by the profusion of rose blooms covering the front wall of our long-house; from one end to the other and from front-yard level to the height of the thatched eaves. I remember the window of my bedroom being fringed with rose blooms for months on end, and the heady scent of the roses permeating the little room. When the weather became chilly, I was always reluctant to close my window fully for that would diminish the scent of the roses. Perhaps it is a throwback to those early years that to this day my favourite scent is the scent of roses. I can never pass a street-vendor selling roses without buying some, whether it be in Cork or in New York.

The roses on that front wall presented a problem when it came to the 'whitewashing'. There were fourteen rose trees in total and each tree was stapled to the wall in several places. After the staples were carefully removed, each tree with its spreading branches was lowered onto the 'floor' of the front yard. Great care had to be taken not to upset the roots of the trees which were set in a neat, narrow bed close to the wall. My grandfather enlisted the aid of my father and mother in this delicate manoeuvre. All three would complain of sore fingers afterwards from the pricking of the thorns. Gardening gloves, as far as country people were concerned, had not yet been invented. So on their hands they wore old, thickly knitted socks, hardened in places from constant darning. Great care was taken to lay the branches (sometimes, depending on the season, laden with blossoms) out along the 'floor' of the front yard. Here they lay, while my grandfather proceeded to coat the wall with wash.

I remember several times as a small child having to carefully pick my steps along the edge of the front yard, trying to avoid stepping on the beautiful rose blossoms. I would always stop when I was safely at the gate and look back to make sure I had not damaged them. It was always amusing to watch the two dogs, Fin and Butcher, high-stepping in very slow motion across the front yard, endeavouring to avoid being pricked by the rose thorns. Sometimes I would hear a little squeal as a thorn went into a paw. Then my grandfather would take the dog and, with a sharp needle borrowed from my grandmother that had been sterilised in boiling water, he would pick out the offending thorn.

For two nights the rose trees were spread on the ground and I would lie awake and worry if the lovely blooms would survive lying on the front-yard floor. But they always did survive, although they were a little droopy when they were first put back in their rightful place against the wall. However, after my father had sprayed them with some potion of his own concoction, some remedy remembered from his training as a bothy-man (gardener), they would quickly revive and stand erect and beautiful on the stems.

There was a two day drying-out period, sometimes longer if rain fell. Then the sensitive procedure of raising the rose trees and restapling each branch to the wall began. More sock-covered hands, more thorn pricks, more muttered curses and then the job was done. The three of them, my mother, my father and my grandfather would stand back across the front yard and admire their handiwork. My grandfather would always say the same thing, 'Thank God that's finished! But, sure, they look lovely against *that* colour on the wall.' No matter what *that* colour was, he would always say the same thing. And, sometimes, just sometimes, the new colour on the wall didn't exactly complement the lovely reds and pale pinks and cream of the roses. In all my years of travelling, it needs only the sight of a rose or the scent of a rose to spark the memory of that multicoloured carpet of living roses spread across the floor of our front yard on 'whitewashing day'.

In a corner of the yard my grandfather had a small, lean-to shed, known to us all as 'The Shack'. This is where he repaired wireless sets; the word 'radio' was not known to us then. As a man of many trades, he specialised in fixing ailing wireless sets. People from every part of the parish took their sets to him to be fixed. But he had an extraordinary *modus operandi*. He would order a part or parts from someone in Tramore. This would usually take a month to arrive. In the interim, with people wanting their sets for some big match, he would 'borrow' parts from one set to fix the set that was urgently needed. After years of this cannibalising of sets, he would be forced to 'loan' a set for a big match. Sometimes it was difficult to recover these 'loaned' sets. People would, understandably, want to hold on to them until their own set was ready.

But after years of this 'robbing Peter to pay Paul', as my grandmother put it, the old man wouldn't know to whom the various sets belonged. There was many a fiery exchange outside the church after Sunday Mass when irate wireless owners demanded that their sets be returned immediately. On the following Wednesday or Thursday, I would be sent in the donkey-cart to deliver a couple of wireless sets. Sometimes they would be promptly returned to say 'this is not mine!' For all the years of my growing up, this running battle of the wireless sets went on, and I never knew how grandfather managed to placate people. I do know that very often on the Sunday of a big match, or sometimes for *Joe Linnane's Question Time*, he would invite several people waiting for their set to be repaired to come to our house and listen to it there. My grandmother and my mother didn't like this for it meant tea and some homemade cakes for the visitors.

I would often visit The Shack and I was always fascinated by the number of sets and the various makes piled up there. On the Friday before a big Sunday match, I would be despatched to Tramore in the donkey-cart with our own battery to have it charged and ready for Sunday's invitees. These Sundays became a kind of social occasion. For a while at least, the heat would be off Grandfather. I never saw any resolution to this problem of the cannibalised wireless sets. The saga just went on and on.

When I was about six years old, I remember a relation, Johnny Connors, who lived in Tramore and worked as a confectioner there, would walk every Sunday to our house in The Glen. He always brought his cocker spaniel with him. He was a lovely friendly man, and his dog was a lovely friendly dog. She was called Libby. We looked forward to his coming, for he always played football with us in the meadow; and he always brought a bag of different kinds of chocolate – Kit-Kat, Aero, Cadbury's Dairy Milk and Rolos. Sunday was like a feast when he came. But mother, in her wisdom, put a lot of the 'goodies' away and gave them to us over the next week. That was seventy years ago and, incredibly, some of those brands are still on the market.

5

The Black and Tans wrecked his bicycle with their rifle butts and broke his two legs, leaving him lying by the roadside. He was found two hours later by a local farmer and he spent three months recovering in hospital. One leg recovered perfectly, but the other didn't; bending the knee was impossible.

From the time I began to really notice things, I wondered why my grandfather always carried a blackthorn stick and walked with a very pronounced limp. And why he was the one person I knew who rode his bicycle using only one leg. At four I didn't have the temerity to ask him directly. So I asked my mother. She told me how the 'accident' to his leg had happened. Back in the early 1920s my grandfather had what was known then as 'an insurance book' to make a little extra money. He was a local agent for an insurance company and collected monthly contributions from holders of small insurance policies in five parishes. This involved a lot of cycling, but he was fit and able for it. He always carried a brown leather bag with his insurance collections in it.

One winter's evening, coming up the big hill in Glenmore, a Crossley tender with Black and Tans aboard stopped him. They began to question him, but when one of them saw the leather bag and looked inside they decided that he was collecting for the 'bloody Republicans'. Nothing he said would convince them he was not. So they 'confiscated' his leather bag and its contents, wrecked his bike with their rifle butts and broke his two legs, leaving him lying on the roadside. He was discovered two hours later by a local farmer and spent three months recovering in hospital. One leg recovered perfectly but the other didn't; the knee never set properly and bending the leg became impossible.

Unable to travel and make his collections, my grandfather had to sell his 'book'. He missed not being able to cycle and began to devise some way to enable him to manage on the bike with his one useful leg. Some of the money he got from the sale of the insurance book went to buy a new

bicycle, lighter than the old one. From this he removed one pedal, which enabled him to let his
bad leg hang down, unimpeded. He fitted a
leather toe-piece to the other pedal into which
he could fit his foot. This made it possible for
him to draw that pedal up, ready for the down-
ward pressure that got the bicycle under way.
However, to attain this mobility with just one leg
required an enormous physical effort and a great
degree of balance and synchronization.

My mother told me that he went into training
on the road outside the house, riding up and
down, up and down, day after day, until he had
mastered the art of riding the bike with one leg.
His biggest problem was mounting and dis-
mounting. He fitted a large flat stone into the
roadside ditch at the gate. His bad leg, which he
could not bend at the knee, was strong enough
to place on this stone, enabling him to mount
the bicycle. From this position he was able to
push off, his bad leg dangling. Hills were a problem; how to dismount at the bottom, enabling
him to walk up pushing his bicycle? And then
how to mount again at the top and continue his
journey? He had two clips on the crossbar of his

bicycle to hold his trusty blackthorn stick.

But he showed tremendous ingenuity in solving this. His main destination was the town of Tramore, three miles away. On this run there were three upward gradients on the outward journey and two on the homeward run. My grandfather, with his friend 'The Gusher', went in the cart drawn by Paycock's predecessor, a donkey named Gander, to each spot where a stepping stone was needed. Armed with pickaxe, spade and suitable flat stones, they fitted the stones into the ditch at the bottom and top of each gradient.

This arrangement was very satisfactory for the journey there and back, but when he reached the main street in Tramore on the outward journey, his troubles really began. Tramore is a very hilly little town and finding a 'landing place' or a 'take-off platform' was not as easy as putting a flat stone in a ditch. After much reconnaissance up and down the steep streets, the odd couple – The Gusher and my grandfather – located three sites as possible 'landing' and 'take-off' places. These were duly tested to satisfy the exacting standards of the two experts. The first was quickly eliminated when my grandfather fell off his bicycle twice, the footpath being too high. Nothing daunted, the indomitable pair went on to test the other two locations. One proved to be on a street that was too steep and so deemed unsafe for 'take-off'.

The third spot, however, though situated on the main street was, by a very happy chance, directly outside a doctor's surgery. The footpath was the correct height, the gradient just right and the medico, Dr Penrose, happened to be my grandfather's GP. The good doctor also happened to be my grandfather's fishing companion most weekends when they fished from the old man's little sailboat. Dr Penrose, being made aware of the situation, was glad to help. He had a neat wooden plaque painted and screwed into the side of the footpath. It said, 'Reserved for Disabled Patient of Dr Penrose.' No pony and cart, no horse and trap, no bicycle ever parked there again. Occasionally some belligerent, argumentative farmer was set to do so but was instantly accosted by Dr Penrose's equally argumentative receptionist who vociferously defended the 'landing place'. From the vantage point of her desk, beside the window of the front office of the surgery, Miss Nora Murphy ruled supreme in guarding my grandfather's spot on the elevated footpath. On Fridays, when he came in to 'land' there, passers-by would stop to watch the aplomb with which he performed the feat. Quite often there would be a few hand-claps and shouts of 'Well done, Mickey!'

My grandfather continued to use his modified bicycle until he was eighty years old. He said that 'coming in to land' was becoming too hazardous then and opted for a safer mode of travel, a lovely little trap pulled by his old friend, Paycock. For three years he made his weekly journey to Tramore. Dr Penrose had an iron ring fixed to the wall above the wooden plaque. The ring re-mained there long after the plaque had been re-moved when my grandfather died. It became a favourite tethering place for all manner of horses and donkeys and became known as 'Mickey's spot'. People would be heard to say, when mak-ing an arrangement to meet a friend in town, 'I'll see you at The Caffler's spot.'

6

The old man eschewed pretence in any shape or form. From early boyhood he instilled in me a great dislike of pride, greed and envy. Of the three, his pet hate was greed. For him, greed was the greatest sin – it should be a criminal offence, punishable by imprisonment.

My grandfather was at heart a poet, a philosopher and, in his way, a mystic. He was sensitive, caring and the very best 'neighbour' in The Glen. He was also a man of the soil, blunt in many pronouncements, outrageously, earthily humorous at times, but never hurtful, never offensive. I must have been barely five when I remember having evidence of this earthy humour. He and I were picking blackberries along the margin of a field. Three young fellows from Tramore were picking along the opposite side. They would be known as 'townies' to us. It was getting late in the afternoon and they approached us to ask what time it was. My grandfather took his great silver watch from his waistcoat pocket, looked carefully at it and while putting it back farted loudly four times. The three lads bolted across the field, one saying to the others, 'Oh, God, Jimmy, come on! He's dangerous! He answered us with his arse!' Just one of his many 'natural' abilities was that of being able to fart at will.

However, his greatest penchant was somewhat more polite. It was that of creating a nickname for someone, used in the most humorous but kindly way. In our small parish we had seven Power families, so to help identify them easily some nicknaming was essential. I remember one particular Power family: the father, mother and three sons were obese and constantly saying how they longed to be slim. My grandfather, with great sensitivity, nicknamed them the 'Skinny' Powers. They saw the humour in it and thereafter gloried in the nickname.

Indeed, I remember an occasion when I was a patient in a Dublin hospital and a young doctor came to examine me. One of the nurses had told him that I was from Waterford, from where he too hailed. When I told him what parish I came from, he laughed and said that was his parish also. While I was trying to think which of five families named Power he might be, he came to my rescue. 'There were several Powers in that parish,' he said. 'You might know us better as the "Skinny" Powers.' Indeed I did, for hadn't my grandfather named them that a long time ago.

The old man eschewed pretence in any form. From early boyhood he instilled in me a great dislike of pride, greed and envy. He also taught me that most of the world's troubles came from people not speaking out and saying what they meant and meaning what they said. He thought that there was too much talk sometimes, from politicians mostly; empty promises that were never honoured. Of such he said, 'Talk is cheap but it takes money to buy beer!' However, his pet hate was greed. He never tired of quoting a few lines from a book some relation had sent him from America. The book was *Remaking the World* by an American evangelist, Frank Buchman. The quotation was, 'Suppose everybody cared enough, everybody shared enough, wouldn't everybody have enough? There is enough in the world for everyone's need, but not enough for everyone's greed.' For him greed was the greatest sin. He felt it should be a criminal offence, punishable by imprisonment.

He was the most charitable of men and could never see the sense of having money anywhere – in bank or post office, under the mattress or in your pocket – and not helping out when someone needed it. He also had a social conscience, which kept telling him there must be better methods of helping the needy than this *ad hoc* way. He was always trying out little schemes to help his fellow parishioners financially. For want of real planning and real support they were not very successful. Then one day walking home with me from the village, we met a young man on the road. The young man's father had died that morning. He was absolutely bereft and at his wits' end to know where he would find the money for his funeral expenses. His mother had died just six weeks before, and all the young man's limited savings had gone to pay her funeral expenses. My grandfather was very sympathetic, calmed the young man down and told him he must not worry about the expense. My grandfather agreed to take care of that. We left the young man, and as we walked along, my grandfather began to laugh gently. I remember so well what he said to me.

'Liam, I've nothing in the bank, very little in the post office, so we're down to the bit that's left in the mattress!'

And out of that 'bit left in the mattress' the funeral expenses were paid to the great relief of the young man who assured my grandfather that the money would be paid back. Sometimes the loans were paid back in part if not in full; sometimes they were never paid back. But out of the whole episode came something else. My grandfather had the beginning of a wonderful idea to help people in the parish who, quite often, were without the wherewithal to bury relatives. He would found a society – a kind of mutual society – where members would make a monthly subscription, depending on their means, and be guaranteed the necessary funeral expenses when they were needed.

For two weeks my grandfather, my father and my mother worked non-stop in getting this whole plan off the ground. A letter had to be composed and written and a copy of it sent to every house in The Uplands and The Glen: 51

households in total. This letter outlined why the society was being formed and requested everyone to attend the meeting at which a committee would be elected, rules drawn up and the first subscriptions accepted.

I was only four or five at that time, but years later when my mother told me the story she laughed a little when she remembered how my grandfather had taken sole responsibility for the composing of the letter. He spent nearly a week poring over the various drafts, testing them on my mother, my father and my poor grandmother, who was confined to bed at the time. Afterwards, I would think, from time to time, of the work my grandfather must have given to the project. Many years later, when I went to see a touring production of a Sean O'Casey play, I was to remember the business of the letter. In the play – I think it was *The Shadow of a Gunman* – two denizens of the tenement, both illiterate, worry about who will write a very important letter for one of them. The male character advises the female character to go to one of the upstairs residents, as 'he'll do a fine letter for you, as fine a letter as was ever *decomposed* by man'. All those years later, whenever I think of my grandfather poring over that very important letter, I think of the O'Casey character busily 'decomposing' by candlelight in his dingy tenement room.

When the letters had been copied out and the envelopes addressed, my father and mother and myself then had the task of delivering them. My mother and I took the donkey and trap and my father his bicycle and they were all delivered in two days. There was an incredible response: forty-eight of the fifty-one families sent a representative to the inaugural meeting. Forty-four of them made a subscription depending on their means. Four of them were indigent but wanted it on record that they supported the idea and would make a contribution when they could. Their good intent was noted in the minutes of the meeting and they were duly, on my grandfather's word, elected full members of the society.

A committee was elected, but finding a name for the society was to prove difficult. Various names were suggested: some were dismissed out of hand; others were put to a vote and defeated. Ultimately, my grandfather suggested a name which was agreed, unanimously, to be the one adopted. The name was The Purgatorial Society. I once asked him, not long before he died, in what divine reservoir of his imagination he discovered that name. He didn't really surprise me by saying, with one of his most impish, enigmatic smiles, that it had come to him 'in a flash' and he just liked the way it sounded. I was reminded of that coming to him 'in a flash' many years later when talking one day to Aeronwy Thomas, Dylan's daughter. She said that her father once told her, in answer to a question she had asked about how a poem started, that it happened 'in a blaze of light'. The Purgatorial Society worked well for several decades, continuing long after my grandfather had died. Eventually, as the people of The Glen and The Uplands grew more prosperous and better organised, it ceased to be needed anymore.

The Purgatorial Society held a general meeting every six months. There was always a great commotion in the house in the week before this meeting, as my grandfather wrote up the big ledger for presentation to the committee. He prided himself on his fine 'hand'. Indeed, it was he who taught me how to write with the same fine 'hand' as himself when I was about six. I remember on the run-up to one meeting he had been very ill and unable to enter up the ledger himself, though he would be able to attend the meeting. He entrusted the task to me, then aged eight, on the basis that having taught me how to write well, I could make the entries in a fine calligraphic hand as good as his own. I was fearful of letting the old man down but, nevertheless, undertook the job. I laboured over the task every evening after school for four evenings. During that time grandfather never once came to look at what I was doing; he trusted me to get on with it.

When I had finished he sat and checked over my work very carefully. When he was done he put his arm round my shoulders and smiled and said, 'Sure you did it as well as if I did it myself. Thank you, Liam. 'Tis so well done the committee won't ever know I didn't do it myself.' And the way he said that made me feel that it meant a lot to him that my young hand so closely resembled his own. He then gave me a half-crown for myself, the most I'd got for any job up to then. But more important than the monetary reward, he gave me a great love of good hand-writing which has never left me. After that, as grandfather's health began to deteriorate, I wrote up the big ledger every half year, always to his complete satisfaction. He was generous and fair and my remuneration for the job was increased to five shillings.

Ever since then I have had a real love of good handwriting. I have never and will never use a biro pen. For me it is always a good old-fash-ioned fountain pen, with a good nib. The biro and the biro-type pen have been the ruination of good handwriting. In all my years I have rarely seen a hand you could call a 'fine hand'. For my-self, I have tried to maintain the quality of my hand; at seventy-eight years of age I write in the same style as that which I used all those years ago to enter up The Purgatorial Society ledger. At every possible opportunity I rail against the use of the biro and feel really upset when I see what passes for handwriting from so many well-educated, professional people. By and large the totally unintelligible squiggle which passes for handwriting on doctors' prescriptions astounds me. I often wonder how the unfortunate chemist manages to decipher the scrawl.

In this day of the computer and email, the handwritten letter is a rarity. But I try to write by hand whenever I can. Nothing gives me greater pleasure than to have someone, to whom I have written, write me in return and comment on the 'lovely handwriting'. I feel no pride then, just a great satisfaction that I help keep alive the great tradition of the good old calligraphic hand. And I always remember my grandfather and that big, old Purgatorial Society ledger. That too, with many another memento, gathers the dust of the years in my attic. However, the memory of it is always with me; the memory of all those entries made in the lovely calligraphic hand that was my grandfather's. And, in my mind's eye, I am hard-pressed to find where the old man's entries ended and mine began.

7

*But first there was the family
rosary. To me, until I was six or seven
years old, the invocation at the end
always seemed to be 'God bless all
our elephants and friends'. For
a long time I wondered where we
kept 'our elephants' but never
had the temerity to ask.*

My grandfather was well read, but his reading often depended on what books he was given by his parish priest. Because he had married a parish priest's housekeeper there was always a strong connection to the clergy. For many years he had given a couple of days every month to keeping the garden of our local parochial house neat, trimmed and tidy. His monetary recompense for this was small, but every month, appreciating how much he liked reading, the parish priest gave him two or three books on loan.

The priest, in a helpful way, usually decided which books my grandfather should read. But occasionally the old man decided for himself. Looking over the priest's bookshelves, if he happened to say that he liked a particular book very much, then the priest would tell him to take it and keep it. In this way he accumulated a tiny library of his own; forty or so titles which were accommodated in the kitchen, on fine wooden shelving, screwed onto the wall beside the big Welsh dresser. My father, knowing how much his books meant to the old man, took time and trouble to seek out some fine pieces of old mahogany and construct the shelving. Hardly an evening went by when he didn't take down one of those treasured books to quote a few lines or to read a poem for me as we sat at the big open fire.

But first there was the family rosary. Every evening immediately after tea at seven o'clock whoever was in the house was expected to kneel for the rosary. Our kitchen table was attached to an iron bar fixed to the wall and could be folded up against the wall when not in use. This gave floor space near the fire for people to kneel. It was considered de rigeur, that fifteen-minute kneel on the hard, flagged floor, the ultimate test of knees and will that sent the strongest shifting uneasily from one knee to the other after five minutes. The elders in the family – grandfather, grandmother, mother and father – took it in turn to lead the prayers, known, why I have no idea, as 'giving out the rosary'. They intoned the various mysteries and the rest of us followed with the responses, the mantra-like drone threatening sleep on all but the most dedicated. Halfway through, I always thought the drowsy drone sounded like the droning of the bees round the beehives in our haggard in high summer.

To round the whole procedure off, we had what were known as 'the trimmin's'. The trimmin's were short prayers for various intentions – a sick animal, fine weather for crops, the success of the parish football team in an upcoming match. There seemed to be no end to the ever-changing litany of requests. But there was one prayer at the end which never changed and which always puzzled me as to its meaning and relevance. It was always delivered by the person who had intoned or 'given out' the prayers, and it was always in a jaded, sleepy monotone that slurred the words. To me, until I was six or seven years old, the invocation always seemed to be, 'God bless all our *elephants* and friends.' For a long time I wondered where we kept 'our *elephants*' but never had the temerity to ask.

One evening, while mending fences along the riverbank with my grandfather, I blurted out, 'Granda, where do we keep the elephants?' The old man seemed surprised and asked me if I knew what an elephant was and how big it was. Hesitantly, I ventured that I had seen pictures of elephants and they were very big. Bigger than Paycock, the old donkey. He then asked me where I got the idea that we 'kept elephants'. I explained about the prayer for 'all our *elephants* and friends'. The old man laughed long and heartily before explaining that the prayer was for 'all our *relatives* and friends'. He said he would talk to the elders about being 'clearer in their speech' when 'givin' out' the trimmin's', conveniently forgetting that he regularly 'gave them out' himself. Perhaps he did talk to them. If he did it made no difference. The invocation still sounded like 'all our *elephants* and friends'. But it was reassuring to know that we had no elephants. It would save me the trouble of looking in all kinds of out-of-the-way places for a space big enough to hide an elephant.

8

Over seventy years later I can still feel the fine, white, warm dust between my toes and the gentle touch of Mary Rose's hand as she led me along.

I remember that morning so well. The April sun was warm and the furze was bright gold on each side of the roadway. High above, so high I couldn't see them, song-drunk larks were soaring under the great blue vault of the sky.

A few weeks after my fourth birthday, I went to school for the first time. I went, as all children in The Glen did, for the last two weeks of the old term before the break for summer holidays. This was calculated to engage the interest of the new pupil, whet the appetite, and in many cases it did. But in many cases it achieved the opposite; some newcomers cried every morning for the two weeks and didn't want to go back in September. For myself, I loved school at the start and hated to think of the long wait until it reopened.

For that two-week introduction each new pupil had a 'carer'. This 'carer' was someone from sixth class who accompanied the new-comer to and from school, introducing the awe-stricken neophyte to the place. So it had to be someone who lived in the same area. I was fortunate to have a girl called Mary Rose Kelly, who lived just across The Glen from us and who called for me every morning.

She seemed frighteningly efficient to me, checking my schoolbag to see that I had my lunch and whatever else I needed on that first day. She also checked me over to see if I 'looked alright'. This 'looked alright' bit was the bit that enraged my mother, as she had taken great trouble over my appearance. As I heard her tell my father that evening, she 'didn't need Tonsil Kelly's daughter to vet me'. Tonsil was a decent man and a great neighbour. He sang in the church choir with my mother. He had been nick-named 'Tonsil' by my grandfather because of his fine tenor voice.

Unlike my mother, I warmed to Mary Rose from the start. Before the end of the two weeks, I had fallen in love with this ultra-efficient, pre-cocious girl, just five years older than myself. She called that first morning with the laces of her shoes tied together and the shoes hung round her neck. It had long been the custom in The Glen that, come spring, children shed their shoes walking to school to save shoe leather. As I was the first from our house for many years to start school, my mother had forgotten about this. There was a great commotion while my poor mother apologised. Mary Rose quickly had my shoes off, the laces tied together and slung round my neck. Then, taking my hand in hers, we were off, up the white, dusty road that led over Cheasty's Hill to the schoolhouse, half a mile away.

Over seventy years later, I can still feel the fine, white, warm dust between my toes, and the gentle touch of Mary Rose's hand as she led me along. I remember that morning so well. The April sun was warm and the furze was bright yellow on each side of the road. High above us, so high I couldn't see them, song-drunk larks were soaring under the great blue vault of the sky. Mary Rose began to sing in Irish, '*Óró sé do bheatha 'bhaile*' as we strolled along. She insisted very gently that I sing along with her. Before we reached the top of the hill, I had learned the first two lines, up to '*anois ag teacht an tSamhraid*'. It was a great feeling. I knew the summer was coming. I was going to school for the first time. I was being cared for by Mary Rose, and I was happy. I remember skipping a little in the hot dust and the skin of my bare feet tight as a drum. And Mary Rose smiled at me and skipped along too.

That first day at school, looking back at it now across the long, long bridge of the years, was one of the most wonderful days of my life. I could never have imagined a place as colourful as the little classroom into which Mary Rose took me, finding me a desk beside a window with a great view of the Comeragh Mountains. The walls of the classroom were covered with so many brightly coloured pictures, such as I had never seen before. I asked Mary Rose what they were. She told me they were maps of all the different countries in the world. I think that I decided, right there and then, aged four, that I would one day travel and see them all.

On the way home that evening, Mary Rose surprised me by telling me that she would be going away to boarding school at the end of summer. I was sad but tried not to show it. Mary Rose was too nice; you couldn't be sad around someone like her. So when we came halfway down Cheasty's Hill and could see the big pool where the stream flowed under the bridge beside our house, I held her hand tightly and started to run. Our shoes, slung round our necks, bobbed wildly as we gained speed with the fall of ground. Together we ran right down and splashed into the cool water. It was so lovely to feel it wash the hot, fine dust from our bare feet. As we stood there, ankle deep in the pool, I looked up and saw our four cats sprawled on the parapet of the bridge, half asleep in the hot sun. They had come to welcome us home. It had been a wonderful day, the only cloud that of Mary Rose going away to boarding school.

I thought I would see Mary Rose when she came home on holiday at the end of her first term at boarding school. I didn't, though, for Mary Rose never came home to The Glen again. She had, my mother told me, 'entered the convent' and was going to become a nun. I didn't see her again for thirty years. She had become a nun in a very strict contemplative order, the Carmelites. For several years she was based in Galway. Then we heard from her father, old Tonsil, that she had been sent to a Carmelite convent in upstate New York. Years later when I worked in New York, I made the journey upstate to see her. She was now Prioress of the convent. Over the years the very strict Rule of the Order had been relaxed, and she was now allowed visitors.

Mary Rose, Sister Veronica in religion, and I spent most of that day together. I had lunch and tea with her at the convent. We talked and talked. She was the same Mary Rose in many ways, her eyes dancing with the same 'devilment' as when we ran down Cheasty's Hill holding hands and waded into the pool beside the little bridge. She remembered all that and my first day at school. But the years in the convent had given her a certain very lovely gravitas. She talked about several radio documentaries I had made for RTÉ, copies of which her father had sent her. She talked in particular about those on Thomas Merton and Dylan Thomas. She loved them and played them often. Before I left she made me promise to come back again soon. I promised I would. But I never got an opportunity to do that. Three months after my visit, Mary Rose died rather suddenly as a result of an inoperable brain tumour.

Back to those early days: I was to spend the next six years at that little national school. They were the only good experiences I had of formal education. It was a two-teacher school. The first two years were spent in what was termed Babies – the first year in Low Babies, the second in High Babies. In those early years I had a dear, kindly, loveable old lady as my teacher, Margaret O'Leary. Miss O'Leary worked tirelessly, with very little help from the Department for Education, to stimulate our young minds. In the classroom she taught us all she could from the limited range of books and educational aids at her disposal. Outside the classroom, when the weather permitted, she took us on walks along the edge of the bog.

I can see her now in my mind's eye armed with her big book, *Bog Flowers and Wild Flowers*, crouched low beside a bog-pool, identifying the various flowers for us, picking samples to take back to the classroom. I also remember her excitement one fine March morning when she announced that she had just acquired a new book, *Life in the Bog Pools*. That very afternoon, all twelve of us, High and Low Babies, were in the heart of the bog examining the pools, our beloved old teacher dipping the little net bag on the long-handled pole into the dun-coloured water. She lifted out all manner of wriggling things and held them in the net long enough for us to examine them. She then made rapid little sketches of each one before 'dipping' them back into their pool again. Afterwards, sitting beside a pool, we would eat our picnic lunch to the music of high-flying larks and unseen grasshoppers lisping in the long dry stalks of the bog-cotton grass while she assiduously made her notes. Her 'field notes' she always called them. Then when we had finished eating our frugal repast of bread and a bottle of milk, she would produce a large bag of her 'special home-made biscuits'. A treat, she said, for being so well-behaved. Ah, days of sun and bog-pools and wriggly, creepy-crawly things – and innocence!

Long after those early schooldays, when I had moved away from The Glen to work in Waterford and Dublin, I would call to see her on my visits home. She would always make a great occasion of my visit, fussing about getting afternoon tea ready. And when I had started to broadcast regularly on RTÉ radio, she loved to discuss some of my latest broadcasts with me. I was, among other things, broadcasting on *Sunday Miscellany* at that time, and many of the talks for that programme were born out of my tea-time chats with her. On one of these visits she told me that her only brother, Fr Dermot, had died in Yorkshire. She reminded me, though I did not need reminding, of all the happy times when I served her brother's morning Mass when he came home for his summer holiday. I remembered those time very well. Fr Dermot, then in his late sixties, liked to sleep on a bit in the mornings. It was after ten o'clock when he came to the church to say Mass. My old teacher always asked her school principal to allow me time off to serve that Mass.

Fr Dermot was a lovely, gentle man with a tremendous knowledge of books. Very often after his Mass, he and I would sit on the steps of the sacristy basking in the summer sun. He would tell me of the books he was reading and had read. He was always interested in the kind of books I was reading and was sometimes surprised at my choices. I had to explain that, in a parish as small as ours, I had very little choice. I had to take what chance and the kindness of others brought me. Every summer, at the end of his month's holiday, he would give me a £5 note, a veritable fortune for an eight-year-old boy. And after his last holiday at home, he gave me a present of a beautifully bound, hardback copy of *Chesterton's Essays*. Three weeks later he died in Yorkshire of a heart attack.

He did not, as I had thought, come back to Ireland to be buried. He preferred to stay in Yorkshire among the people he had worked with for thirty years. The first thing I think of when I think of Fr Dermot is a saying of Thoreau's, which he often quoted to me sitting on those sacristy steps so long, long ago, 'We must learn to reawaken and keep ourselves awake, not by mechanical aid, but by an infinite expectation of the dawn.'

I was working in South America when my old teacher died, aged ninety-eight. I was told her funeral was the best attended for many years; several generations of ex-pupils, parents and grandparents came to pay their respects.

The other teacher in that school was a man, Michael Donaghy. He was principal and he taught me for four years. Four wonderful, glorious years when he opened my mind to all the possibilities there were in the big world. He always talked to us 'plain', as he put it himself. He told us that he was just a facilitator, someone to help us go on to do what we really wanted to do in life. He sometimes joked about being a kind of John the Baptist. Above all else he encouraged us to read and read and read. That was long before the advent of travelling libraries, so he built up, at his own expense, a wonderful little library of good books in the school. Over his years at that school he turned out several generations of boys and girls, some of whom went on to become priests, doctors, nurses and vets. Others went on to work the farms on which they had grown up, while a few, as will always be the case, opted out of life, emigrated and ended in the gutters of London, Birmingham and Manchester. And one, a classmate and close friend of mine, had a very special life.

Only when Michael Donaghy died rather tragically did I discover that he was an alcoholic. I thought then of all those years of his helping, his kindness, his facilitating. Years when none of us even suspected he had a problem. He was married and had his home in another village twenty miles away. All of his working life he lived in lodgings in the town of Tramore from Monday to Friday, cycling to and from our little school. He then took the bus home on Friday evening and back again on Sunday night. It must have been a lonely life for him, living like that from Monday to Friday. He was a very quiet, shy man, gentle and retiring. He would sometimes let slip in class a comment about how lonely it was living away from home during the working week. This loneliness must have helped make him a quiet, addictive drinker during the week in Tramore.

I was at boarding school when my mother wrote to tell me of the 'poor Master's death'. It was early December; autumn weather with heavy frosts, bitingly cold. Apparently, on the evidence of some acquaintances in Tramore, it was his wont after a few drinks to take a constitutional walk along the promenade every night before going to his lodgings. He was found unconscious by some early morning walker in one of the little shelters along the way. Rushed to hospital, he died there some few hours later of heart failure, induced by hypothermia.

The Master was one of the great influences in my young life, sowing the seed and then cultivating positive, independent thinking. He it was who saw in me at age eight or nine the potential to write well. From that age he encouraged me to write little stories. Those first stories were written in Irish and published in an 'occasional' magazine brought out by a group of Irish speakers from Ring, the Waterford Gaeltacht. The magazine was 'occasional' in the sense that its publication depended on the availability of funding. He submitted them for me, and he was positively beaming with pride that 'one of my boys' had made it into print. Often, since then, when I've published a book or presented a radio talk or documentary, I've thought of him and the great part he played in shaping my thought. I think of how instrumental he was in giving me that independence of spirit, that never-take-no-for-an-answer attitude to life. I still treasure a copy of Thoreau's *Walden* which he gave me when I was going to boarding school. That copy of *Walden* is still one of my few bibles; one of the beacons by which I endeavour to steer a safe passage through the vicissitudes of life.

9

*And somewhere in those lovely meadow
lands between Medford and Concord,
I would lose Paul Revere and fall
asleep. The little candle of my
consciousness would be burned out, and
my father would carry me off to bed; my
subconscious still filled with the sound
of Paul Revere's horse galloping
on and on into the dark.*

I was five at the time and had started school
when my grandfather introduced me to the magical world of Longfellow's *Tales of a Wayside Inn*.
I would curl up beside him in the warmth of the
inglenook as he intoned the opening lines of
'The Prelude':

> One Autumn night, in Sudbury town,
> Across the meadows, bare and brown,
> The windows of the wayside inn
> Gleamed red with firelight, through the
> leaves
> Of woodbine hanging from the eaves,
> The crimson curtains rent and thin.

I loved the meadows being 'bare and brown' and the windows gleaming 'red with firelight'. But best of all the tales told in that old inn, I loved 'Paul Revere's Ride'. I would pull at my grandfather's sleeve shouting, 'Ride! Ride! The Ride!' and he would laugh and tease me, 'Can't find Paul Revere tonight, Liam! Think he must be gone fishin'!' But eventually he would open the book, settle himself in a comfortable position and take up the long poker from its place against the hob. Then, after he had raked the glowing embers, out would come, in that sonorous voice I knew and loved so well, the first rousing lines of the poem. I would jog in my inglenook seat in great excitement, riding the ride with Paul Revere.

> Listen, my children, and you shall hear
> Of the midnight ride of Paul Revere.
> On the eighteenth of April, in Seventy-five,
> Hardly a man is now alive
> Who remembers that famous day and year.

I was with Paul as he left the Charlestown shore. With him as he climbed the steps of the old North Church Tower and hung his lantern aloft. Still with him as he galloped through Lexington, but my consciousness was slowly dumbing down to the drumming of his horse's hooves. I was very sleepy then and by Medford my eyes were beginning to close, starting to flicker like a candle that had reached its end. And, somewhere, in those lovely meadow lands, between Medford and Concord, I would lose Paul Revere and fall asleep. The little candle of my consciousness would be burned out, and my father would carry me off to bed; my subconscious still filled with the sound of Paul Revere's horse galloping on and on into the dark night, calling on all those farm folk to rise and fight the English.

Next day, I would put on my 'Paul Revere hat' and buckle on my belt and wooden sword and ride a long-handled old farmyard broom around the meadow, through Charlestown and Medford, Lexington and Concord. Charleston was the Meadowstone, Medford a little pile of stones beside the stream, Lexington a wooden stake sunk in the bank a little further on and Concord an old lean-to shelter for Paycock and the two cows at the far end of the meadow. The old donkey would watch my antics in silent amusement for a while and then begin a loud hee-hawing. The two cows, Sam and Sadie, would run around the end of the meadow, kicking their heels and 'mooing' all the while, obviously entering into the spirit of my mad charade.

My grandfather insisted that I repeat the opening words of the poem after him so that I could recite, word perfect, the first dozen lines of 'Paul Revere's Ride'. Longfellow's 'Song of Hiawatha' I loved also, but I found the Indian names difficult, so difficult that I could never even begin to memorise any of the lines.

There were several other Longfellow poems that I remember from those very early days. Indeed Longfellow was then, and still is, one of my favourites. One of my most loved poems was 'The Village Blacksmith'. I had gone several times with my grandfather to have Paycock's shoes replaced by the blacksmith at the top end of our glen. Standing there watching Paddy 'Buck' Power, the blacksmith, about his work, I always remembered Longfellow's lines:

> And children coming home from school
> Look in at the open door:
> They love to see the flaming forge,

And hear the bellows roar,
And catch the burning sparks that fly
Like chaff from a threshing floor.

Sometimes when I walked with grandfather on the beach and the sea was high and the big breakers crashed against the rocks with a frightening roar, I would ask him to tell me about 'The Wreck of The Hesperus'. And shouting above the roar of the sea and the wind, he would recite some of Longfellow's wonderful lines…

It was the schooner *Hesperus*,
That sailed the wintry sea;
And the skipper had taken his little daughter,
To keep him company.
Then the maiden clasped her hands and prayed
That saved she might be:
And she thought of Christ who stilled the wave,
On the lake of Galilee.
And fast through the midnight dark and drear,
Through the whistling sleet and snow,

Like a sheeted ghost the vessel swept
Tow'rds the reef of Norman's Woe.

After that the old man's voice would trail off
and he would stop to rest. I would stand and look
out to sea and imagine the schooner out there,
riding the big waves. That line 'Tow'rds the reef
of Norman's Woe' always gave me a funny, shiv-
ery feeling, and I asked my grandfather why the
reef was called Norman's Woe. Much to my surprise he had to admit he didn't know. He was not
a man who didn't have answers to most of the
questions with which I plagued him. I loved so
many of those old poems, but always my greatest
love was Paul Revere. That night, snug in the inglenook, the big fire blazing, the crickets singing
unseen in the hob, I would listen to 'Paul Revere's
Ride' and between the verses think of the skipper's little daughter dying in the great storm.

Many years later travelling in the USA, I had
the good fortune to visit that lovely countryside
through which Paul Revere made that historic
ride. From Boston through Medford, Lexington
and Concord. I visited the original Wayside Inn,
then beautifully, tastefully refurbished by the
Henry Ford Foundation and still functioning as

an inn. And just half a mile down the road from the inn was the schoolhouse to which, in fact, Mary took her little lamb (the poem was inspired by Mary Sawyer, who really did bring her pet lamb to this very schoolhouse). It was still preserved as a schoolhouse, but one of the rooms had been fitted as a kitchen where the muffins used at the inn were baked every day. This was the same schoolhouse I had first heard about as a three-year-old, when my mother read the story to me. I still remember the sound of my mother's soft voice and see the coloured pictures in the book from which she read:

> Mary had a little lamb, its feet were white as snow,
> And everywhere that Mary went the lamb was sure to go.
> It went with her to school …

I also remember the hurt look on my mother's face when I came home from school one day and recited a few lines of the latest 'variation' I'd heard in the playground on Mary and her little lamb.

Mary had a little lamb, its feet were black as soot
And into Mary's pot of jam, one sooty foot it put ...

She stopped me there and said I should be ashamed of myself making fun of Mary and her little lamb. I did recite it again, but never in her presence.

On that visit to America I couldn't help thinking how great it would have been if my grandfather and my mother were still alive and I could have written and told them. I feel sure that my mother all those years ago never thought of Mary and her little lamb as anything but a story, never thought of it as being a true story.

My grandfather, had he lived, would have been so pleased to get a letter from me telling him that I had visited that wonderful country through which Paul Revere rode. He would have shown it, not to boast, just as 'a matter of fact' to all his old friends as they sat round the fire in our big flag-floored kitchen. For that was where they would first have heard the *Tales of a Wayside Inn* at one of our Open Nights when my grandfather read them to me. And they would all have been pleased that 'one of their own' had visited such an historic place and written to tell them about it.

10

He would regale us with a story, during the telling of which you could hear the silence hanging like a halo round the telling of the tale. And then at the end of the story, with a great flourish, Snooks would whip a battered mouth organ from his pocket and play something soft and low from his great repertoire of O'Carolan melodies — Snooks was indeed a man for all seasons.

The Open Nights at our old long-house near the cliff top, where the three dusty roads met, were famous, not just in the parish but far beyond. Our big kitchen was a Mecca for all the best musicians, singers, story-tellers and dancers from six parishes. On Wednesday nights a crowd of twenty or more of them would crowd into our kitchen and the flag floor and rafters would ring with their performances. But there would be little islands of quiet while Snooks Hayes and my grandfather, and some other old *seanchaí*, would hold us all in thrall with some grand story. From the time I was five or six I was allowed to stay up to hear and see some of these wonders. I would snuggle in the inglenook, close to my grandfather, and battle with sleep. I often marvel that now, at seventy-seven years of age, I battle with sleep in the very same way as when I was seven years old, and lose the battle, as I did then, every time.

Looking back now, through cataract-clouded eyes, I remember many of these performers. Some I can fit names to. The Hayes brothers, so different in appearance and personality. Big six-foot-six Snowball and Snooks, his older brother, five-foot-seven or eight, who always wore his trademark cap: an old cloth cap turned back to front, which gave him a rakish look that perfectly suited his ebullient personality. Snooks would sing and dance, his metal-studded boots striking sparks from the old flag floor. He would regale us with a story, during the telling of which you could hear the silence hanging like a halo round the telling of the tale. And then at the end of the story, with a great flourish, he would whip a battered mouth organ from his pocket and play something soft and low from his great repertoire of O'Carolan melodies, something sad and evocative that moved and cheered us. For as Francis Ledwidge said of his old friend the fiddler Matt McGoona, 'He would come when we were all feeling low and cheer us with sad music.' Well, that was exactly what Snooks did – cheered us with sad music. 'Planxty Fanny Poer' and 'Planxty Irwin' were his favourites and ours. His movements were not graceful – legs dangling and gangling, arms akimbo. Snooks always ended by laying down a challenge. He would hold his hands above his head, bash his metal-studded boots on the floor and shout, 'Follow that!'

And his brother, Snowball, always 'followed that'. He would sing and then dance. He had a fine baritone voice and would regale us with 'The Harp That Once', 'I Dreamt I Dwelt', 'Danny Boy' and many other popular songs. His dancing was a treat to watch. A big man, he moved as if his feet were barely touching the floor, gliding noiselessly over the flag surface as if he were dancing on water, his head high, every movement perfect. So different was he in every way from Snooks that it was difficult to believe they were blood brothers. With Snowball there was no histrionic posturing, no dramatic flourish at the end. He would smile and bow graciously and leave the floor to the next performer.

With so many fine performers there was bound to be a competitive spirit evident. My grandfather would have nothing of this. He was against competition between artists, for to him they were all artists, all unique, and the whole idea of being in competition with each other odious. Most accepted the 'house rule' without demur, but occasionally, in silent protest, someone never came back again. 'Better off without them,' my grandfather would say philosophically.

There would always be a firkin or two of porter in the house on these occasions. Whether it was one or two depended on the ability of the participants to put money in the communal kitty on the particular night. Very often on a night when one firkin seemed the limit, my grandfather and my father would purchase a second. This was done on the basis that 'performing was a thirsty business and no performer should be parched'.

These sessions were always noisy, always high-spirited but never rowdy. I would sit in the inglenook with my grandfather until my eyes dimmed and I began to fall asleep. Then my father would take me in his arms and put me to bed. It was difficult to settle down then, for I could hear the music and dancing, albeit muffled now, and so I lay awake for a long time before drifting into sleep. And when I did sleep it was a restless sleep, the huge seas of my dreams washing over me, great waves of music and song carrying me to places I had never seen before, and would never see again. Sometimes, between dreams, I would get out of bed and go to the window that looked out on the meadow. On clear-skied, starry nights I could just see the outline of the Meadowstone. Through the noise coming from our kitchen I could hear the swish and gurgle of the stream as it swept past. When it wasn't cold, I would climb onto the window ledge and sit there and imagine all the adventures the fairies were getting up to in the dark. And in summer and early autumn, the scent of the roses climbing round the window would add to my drowsiness and I would fall asleep curled up on the wide window ledge.

11

*I loved the sweet pungent odour
of the incense in the thurible at
benediction. I loved the deep resonant
sound of the bell on the altar steps
when it was struck with the soft-
headed drumstick, especially at the consecration when the church was hushed.*

The happiest time of my childhood was, without doubt, the time spent as an altar boy in the parish church. Those never-to-be-forgotten years took place from the age of seven to eleven when my whole existence was centred on serving Mass and benediction and attending at funerals and weddings. I particularly loved the responses in Latin at the Mass. I loved the sweet, pungent odour of the incense in the thurible at benediction. I loved the deep resonant sound of the bell on the altar steps when it was struck with the soft-headed drumstick, especially at the Consecration when the church was hushed. I loved holding the shining gold plate, walking before the priest as he distributed Holy Communion to the people kneeling at the altar rail. I secretly wished that just once someone would let the little round, sacred bread fall on the plate, so that I could show how well I would handle that situation. But not once in those four years did that happen.

I was very fortunate that my time working as an altar boy coincided with the ministry of Fr Jim Sullivan. He was a big man, middle-aged; a man of great energy and imagination, who had the great gift of making the most impossible projects come to fruition. He was a man who never took no for an answer. He was a man who'd got his values right, his priorities straight. Shortly after he came to the parish, the old widow, Maggie Power, who looked after the sacristy and the priest's vestments, ventured to suggest that the one set of vestments fit for everyday use was threadbare and needed replacement. He asked her to check out the cost of a new set of vestments and also to check how much was in the church fund, adding that he had a few sums of his own to do.

Ten days later Maggie presented Fr Jim with the figures: there would be just enough in the fund to cover the cost of the vestments. Fr Jim said that the amount in the fund would just about cover the cost of confirmation outfits for some needy children in the parish. He then got Maggie to lay out the worn vestments and examined them carefully with her. He told her very gently, with a big smile, that if she trimmed away the gilt stuff which was frayed, the green cloth was quite fresh underneath and would do fine for another while. Maggie was very impressed. She had been used to a succession of parish priests who were very conscious of their station and would have insisted on getting new vestments. She was a lady who had the ear of the whole parish, so news of Fr Jim's charitable gesture spread quickly.

Fr Jim it was who extolled the virtues of simplicity and humility from the pulpit every Sunday. He rarely let a Sunday go by without reference to Jesus as the 'Humble Nazarene' – gentle, comforting, all forgiving. This greatly surprised my parents and my grandparents who, when clericalism at its worst was rampant, had been browbeaten by a succession of parish priests and missioners into the belief that Jesus was vengeful and unforgiving. It was difficult for these older people in The Glen to accept this 'Humble

Nazarene'. However, in due time they did. When I was growing up they had so accepted the concept that a stranger coming into The Glen might be forgiven for thinking that the Humble Nazarene lived in the next-door farm.

And in a sense he did. He lived in every household. It was not unusual round the table at mealtimes or round the fire at night to hear one family member upbraid another with the remark, 'And what would the Humble Nazarene think of that?' It was a tribute to Fr Jim's ability to communicate meaningfully that the Humble Nazarene became a living presence in our glen. Indeed, seventy-seven years later, He is a living presence to me. That Humble Nazarene is the God I acknowledge, love and worship.

Every two years there was a mission in the parish. Two priests, so-called expert communicators, came for two weeks and preached to us every night; women one week, men the other. But they talked of a God we didn't know – a haughty, vengeful, uncompassionate God. We still had a pulpit in those days, a wooden one, and it reverberated with the blows of the missioners' hands as they hammered home their message,

'God will not be mocked! God will be avenged!' Some of the older parishioners were confused, endeavouring to reconcile this vengeful, unforgiving God of these fire-and-brimstone preachers with the Humble Nazarene of Fr Jim. After the mission had ended it took the older people a week or two to accept that no reconciliation was possible between the diametrically opposed godheads, and they were happy to continue to follow the Humble Nazarene. After this ripple of temporary clerical disruption, peace descended once more on the little fields of The Glen and the broad fields of The Uplands.

Every morning during the summer holidays I would go beachcombing with my grandfather before going to serve the ten o'clock Mass. I remember particularly the summer of 1940. That was the time of the Battle of Britain, a time when the war impinged on us very noticeably. Then we could hear almost every night the drone of the German Hinkels and Stukas on their way to bomb and strafe Swansea and Cardiff on the Welsh coast. The reverberation of the bombing rattled the delph on our big kitchen dresser. Most mornings there would be interesting flotsam and jetsam to be picked up along the little beach below the house: airmen's caps, document cases, leather jackets and once ... a German airman.

That morning I had gone ahead of my grandfather to search the rock pools. The two dogs gambolled about far up the beach. I saw what I thought to be bleached, white seaweed in a clear pool. As I watched it rise and fall with the motion of the outgoing tide, I realised that it was the blond hair of a man, his body wedged between two large rocks. He must have been a long time in the water; his flesh was badly eroded and where his eyes had been were just deep, black sockets. A little silver chain, hung round his neck, had sunk into the white, eroded flesh. The identification disk which had hung on it was gone, torn off by the savage tides. I stood there petrified until my grandfather caught up with me. I was then sent on my bicycle to the big army camp two miles up the coast to report the find. They removed the body a little later.

There was no way of knowing what the airman's religion was, so Fr Jim decided that the poor fellow should have a proper burial. I was one of the two altar boys with Fr Jim when the body was laid to rest in our little graveyard a few days later. Many such tragedies occurred along our stretch of coast during that time, mostly German. Many years later the German Embassy in Dublin disinterred many bodies, including 'our' airman, and laid them to final rest in the lovely German Cemetery under Featherbed Mountain in Glencree in the Dublin mountains. Since I have come back to Dublin, I visit there every year in July or August when the 'Glen of the Heart' is green and glistening under the sun. A little waterfall cascades down the cliff face and flows along beside the sleeping dead. And away toward the sea, the Sugarloaf Mountain, like a miniature Everest, stands sentinel over all that lovely glen, keeping watch over the war dead. I wonder then as I walk between the rows of little granite crosses which of those marked 'unknown' is my airman. There is a beautifully poignant poem written by Professsor Stan O'Brien engraved on a polished stone near the entrance:

> It was for me to die
> Under an Irish sky;
> There finding berth
> In good Irish earth.

What I dreamed and planned,
Bound me to my fatherland.
But, War sent me
To sleep in Glencree.
Passion and pain
Were my loss, my gain.
Pray as you pass,
To make good my loss.

Fr Jim was a great man for involving himself in various social activities in the parish. He trained the local junior football team for several years and was also very involved in amateur dramatics. He produced two plays every year, one every autumn and one in early spring. Most of the plays had a 'juvenile' part in them and I always got that part. Fr Jim was a fine producer and very ambitious. He toured every production to four satellite parishes within a distance of ten miles. During the war there was no petrol, except a ration for doctors and priests. Now Fr Jim refused to use his ration for anything other than sick calls and giving the doctor a gallon or two to help with his sick calls.

So our props and costumes were all transported by horse and cart. The cast cycled or went by horse and trap. I travelled in reasonable comfort on a little saddle fixed by my father to the cross-bar of Fr Jim's bicycle. Comfortable until one instance when a fierce squall off the sea caught us on the coast road. We arrived sodden to present our mammoth production in a cold village hall. The stage was some planks laid on top of tar barrels, fronted by a tatty black cloth covered with stars. After one of these gigs, the local priest rather arrogantly asked Fr Jim why he worked so hard at this thankless task. Fr Jim hid his chagrin under a very polite reply. He said it gave a lot of pleasure to a lot of people and it raised a few pounds for charity. When the questioner looked suitably chastened, I remember well what Fr Jim said as he laughed, 'And sure why can't we clergy be Irishmen too!'

12

I think I always preferred the nights when just two or three old friends of my grandfather — the regulars — visited and quietly sat, chatted and told stories. And if the mood took them, they might play a tune on fiddle or accordion. On these nights there was no porter, just my mother's very special supper. The first of these regulars was Luke Tarpey, a bachelor farmer from The Uplands.

For all of my childhood that I can recall, one old man came every night, including Sunday, to visit. He was Luke Tarpey, a bachelor farmer from The Uplands. He had been at school with my grandfather and had no family left now apart from the bachelor brother with whom he shared the farm. Indeed that was the only thing they shared — the farm. It was a large farm which, with the help of two hired men, they worked very efficiently. By day they worked very hard side by side, very often working for several days without speaking. By night the brother, Willie, went to the local pub and drank every night until closing time. But Luke came to our house. In a sense, we became his family. He was a great fiddle player. Quiet, retiring, he would never play on the Open Nights. On those nights he sat in his own, special corner beside the fire, on the old wooden settle. That was known as 'Luke's Corner' and whoever occupied it when he arrived, quickly and without demur, found another seat. Not that the old man ever expected it. He would just smile and say, 'Oh, thank you!', as if he had just come in for the first time and somebody had offered him a seat.

Without any doubt, Luke Tarpey was the most widely read man I have ever known. Also, without doubt, he was the most gracious man I have ever known. Though no one ever knew what Luke had worked at in America, he must have undergone some wonderful transformation to become the man he was. As a young man he was known in the parish as 'a bit of a rake', 'a ragamuffin', 'a scallywag', in Irish – a *straicaire*. He had fallen out with his father and gone to

America, where he settled in Boston for nearly twenty years. He returned when his father fell ill and there was a reconciliation. After his father's death he remained at home to share the farm with a bachelor brother. This brother always resented the fact that the returned prodigal was given a half-share in the farm. Luke maintained that all the education anyone needed came from reading, and if it came to a choice between good books and bad teachers, he would take the good books every time. I have no doubt that he, my grandfather and my first teacher at the little national school greatly influenced me in deciding what, for me, education was all about.

Luke was idiosyncratic and eccentric, and he was fortunate to have means enough to indulge his eccentricities. He kept a couple of well-trained, half-breed horses. Every Friday he saddled one and rode the ten miles to Waterford City. On these excursions he carried two capacious leather saddlebags – one for the library books he would borrow from week to week, the other for whatever new or second-hand books he might buy. And in each bag he would manage to accommodate some choice pieces of good cheese, a couple of bottles of wine and whatever other food he needed to gratify the modest epicurean tastes he had acquired during his sojourn in Boston. He introduced me to what he called 'a beautiful smelly cheese' known as Gorgonzola, followed a little later by another 'smelly cheese' called Roquefort. Luke it was, when I was about nine or ten, who showed me how to make a Roquefort dressing, something I still do and enjoy with a good salad. Incredibly for a boy of six, I liked both cheeses and acquired a taste for them that I never lost. From time to time he would take me little pieces of various other cheeses wrapped carefully in greaseproof paper, the names of which I have have long since forgotten. So, unfortunately, I had cultivated a taste for the 'smelly cheese' long before I could afford to buy it.

Old Luke could make his fiddle sing. I say 'his' advisedly for he would never play another person's fiddle nor allow anyone to play his. Jigs and reels, hornpipes and slides he played with great expertise. But like Snooks Hayes, it was O'Carolan he loved best. He would play the wonderful slow airs, a faraway look on his face, as if he was dreaming of Boston and the life he had lived there. A life he very rarely mentioned except sometimes in passing when he would say something like, 'when I was in Boston, I knew a man who boasted that he had killed seven men …'. That would be as far as he went with the story, and he wasn't a man of whom you asked questions. Luke told you as much as he wanted to tell, and that was that. An avid yet fastidious reader, the book he talked most about was F. Scott Fitzgerald's *The Great Gatsby*. He loaned me a copy when I was about ten. Years later I could not help feeling that during his time in Boston he was in some way part of that Gatsby scene.

Luke was the most generous of people. He regularly brought little presents for us from his Friday trips to the city. Chocolates for my mother, cigarettes for my father, snuff for my grandfather, a toy for Michael and a book for me. I still have more than a dozen books dating from that time, the late 1930s, all presents from Luke and all bought in the little second-hand book-shop in Waterford to which he introduced me when I was nine or ten years old.

One night Luke announced, sitting at our fire-side, that he had sold his two half-breeds, as he was getting too old for riding horses now. He was the same age as my grandfather, about seventy-two or seventy-three. To replace them he had bought a trap and a fine mare to pull it. So he would still be making his usual weekly trip to Waterford City. On his first trip the following Saturday, he would like me to accompany him. That was to be my first trip to the city, and though I did not suspect it then, my last for some time.

On that first trip he introduced me to the lady who owned the second-hand bookshop, Miss Gertie Power. She was an elderly lady, shabbily, carelessly dressed, her great mass of grey hair piled like a windswept hay stack. The two things that struck me most on that first acquaintance were her mad blue eyes that darted here and there as she spoke and her obvious love of books. She loved books and she loved the people who loved books. After Luke had introduced me, she told me that she knew my grandfather well. He used to come in regularly up to a few years back. Loved his books, she said. At this point she leaned across the little counter and holding me by my arm, her mad, blue eyes darting about, she half-whispered: 'A great man for finding the nickname, your grandad! Named my family sixty years ago. Called us the "Stickyback Powers".'

She then told me of how her brother, Teddy, had just started working as a street photographer. He worked the promenade in Tramore every summer with the old camera on a tripod and the big black cloth over his head and shoulders. My grandfather saw him one Sunday and next time he was in with her, he told her he'd seen Teddy and mentioned the big black cloth which looked like it was stuck to his back. From then on Teddy was known, not as Teddy Power, but 'Teddy Stickyback' and they were instantly the 'Stickyback Powers'. Her father was furious. But the name wouldn't go away. So for brevity's sake, she became 'Gertie Sticky' and Teddy, still working his camera, became 'Teddy Sticky'. With a broad grin Gertie admitted that despite the initial objection from her family the soubriquet had worked well for them in their respective businesses. It helped to distinguish them from the dozens of unrelated and distantly related Powers in the Waterford area. She seemed genuinely sorry that, as both herself and Teddy had never married and there were no other siblings in the family, the 'Sticky' name would die with them.

That was my introduction to Gertie Sticky. I was destined not to see her again for over a year.

On that first visit, I well remember, Luke bought me a book of my own choice, *The Poetical Works of Robert Burns*. It was a fine old volume with a gold-embossed cover. I still dip into that to find some old poem that half comes into my mind out of the raggle-taggle bag of memories. Sometimes a friend visiting my little work room will see the Burns book and say, 'My God, where did you get that lovely volume?' And it is too long a story to tell them. Now they can read it here.

One night shortly after Christmas, when Luke was in his mid-seventies, he did not visit us. We didn't worry. But when two, three nights went by without a visit, my grandfather walked up across the fields to the Tarpey place. Luke's brother was alone, sitting at the kitchen table with a half-consumed bottle of whiskey before him. Luke had been missing for three days. He, the brother, had searched the farm for Luke, but there was no sign of him. One of the dogs was also missing. He had gone with Luke but neither had returned. My grandfather asked if he had searched 'The Little Streets'. The drunken brother said he had not. My grandfather came home, got our two dogs and, taking me with him, we went to search for Luke.

Now, 'The Little Streets', about half a mile from our house, was the very sparse remains of a small hamlet abandoned during the Famine. A few low walls remained standing and several mounds of stones were now covered with grass and weeds. From early childhood when I first went there with my grandfather, I could sense the place had an eerie feel about it. Luke had often talked about the place. He had located some reference to it in an old history book and often went there with his sheepdog, Win. He said he liked to sit there on one of the old wall-ends to get 'the feel of the place.' He used to joke and say after a visit there, 'Sure, maybe young Liam will write a story about it one day!' And maybe I will someday.

Afterwards, my grandfather said, that when the drunken brother had said that Luke had gone with the dog, Win, he had a premonition that the pair had gone to 'The Little Streets'. He was right. As we approached the ruins we heard a dog bark. Our dogs barked in answer and ran forward. One of them ran back to us whimpering. We found poor Luke lying dead on a mound of stones with Win lying across him and an old history book open beside him. He had died of heart failure and had been lying there for three days. Win had tried to keep him warm by lying on him. Luke Tarpey's dead body was the first I had ever seen. It shocked me. For over a week I wandered about in a stupor. Every night I sat beside my grandfather in the old inglenook and kept looking across the hearth to where Luke's seat was empty. I think I expected him to materialise and sit there smiling and rosining his bow to play us a tune. But of course he didn't materialise, and in time other visitors sat in 'his' seat. At the start I resented this and told them they could not sit there, because that was 'Luke's seat.' But eventually, as with all inevitabilities, I accepted this one.

About a month after we had buried Luke, a letter arrived for my father from a solicitor in Waterford City. This letter stated that 'Mr. Luke Tarpey, Farmer, late of "The Uplands", had left monies in trust to send Liam O'Longain to boarding school, and maintain him there for as long as was considered necessary, or for as long as Liam felt that such "formal education" was of benefit to him.' The letter went on to say that should I decide to leave school at any time, the balance remaining in the trust fund should pass to Henry Long to spend as he thought fit. My father, mother and grandparents were overcome with emotion. It was an emotion born of several things – of Luke's lonely death, of his great generosity and of the fact that I was about to go to boarding school, the first in the family to do that.

But above all else, it was the memories of Luke ensconced in 'his' special chimney corner seat, playing some soft, slow air on his fiddle. Or Luke in his soft, gentle voice telling us of some wonderful old book he had just discovered in Gertie Sticky's bookshop. Or Luke after a visit to Waterford City setting down at our kitchen table a parcel containing a present for everyone in the house. Some High-Toast snuff for my grandfather, cigarettes for my father, chocolates for my mother, jelly sweets for my toothless grandmother and some 'smelly' cheese or a book for me. Whenever Michael was home from hospital he was included. And once, I remember, a month before he died, Luke brought me a magazine called *John O'London's Weekly*. It was, he said, 'written by "real" writers for people who wanted to be "real" writers'.

That magazine opened up a whole new world for me. From the moment I read that first copy,

I knew I wanted to be a writer – a 'real' writer. But it was to be several months before I got to Waterford City, with my grandfather, and found some back-numbers of *John O'London's* in Gertie Sticky's dingy bookshop. And it was to be several years before I went to work and was able to order my own copy every week. I never opened a copy of the magazine without thinking of my great old friend and generous benefactor, Luke Tarpey.

13

The Gusher was the parish gravedigger,
a job he took very seriously. So seriously
that, on occasion, you got the impression
that it was the officiating priest
who assisted The Gusher, not the
other way round. Over a pint in the
local he would regularly let slip
immortal words such as, 'After
Fr Kerrigan and meself said
the Mass before the burial...'

The second regular visitor was The Gusher Hayes, uncle of Snowball and Snooks and my grandfather's best friend. The Gusher was the parish gravedigger, a job he took very seriously. So seriously that, on occasion, you got the impression that it was the officiating priest who assisted The Gusher, not the other way round. He had two outfits. One was his grave-digging outfit; the other was his funeral suit. The gravedigging outfit consisted of an old pair of dungarees and what was once a white Aran sweater. His funeral suit was a black three-piece suit given to him by a curate. After many months of wearing and un-caring it was sad-looking and unpressed, and after many more wearings it had begun to look well past its best. Still, it gave The Gusher a lift when he put it on to 'officiate', as he said himself, at the graveside. Over a pint in the local he would regularly let slip immortal words such as, 'After Fr Kerrigan and myself said the Mass before the burial …' Or during the season of the Stations Masses he would leave the pub early, saying, 'Must have an early night. We're away in The Up-lands in the morning. Meself and Fr Kerrigan are saying the Mass.' In his own estimation The Gusher had attained a certain semi-clerical status in the little community, and so well was the old man liked that nobody ever laughed at him for this or any of his other little foibles. Though his duties in the church were strictly those of gravedigger, he had appropriated to himself the title of 'verger'. He told my grandfather that, in reading a book loaned to him by the parish priest, he had come across the title 'verger'. It was, he said, given to someone in the church who acts as 'an official, caretaker or attendant' and was much more suited to his status than the more lowly designation of gravedigger. The priests and the parishioners, in magnanimous deference to the old man's harmless preference, were happy to accommodate him.

A bachelor, he lived alone in a thatched cottage at the head of The Glen. His only companion in all the years I knew him was his black sheepdog, Digger. He grazed a dozen or so sheep on the hill behind the house and fattened a couple of pigs for his own use. My grandfather, known as the best man in the parish to kill and cure a pig, would oblige The Gusher a couple of times a year. So The Gusher would dine royally on fresh pork for a while and thereafter on cured bacon. The sheep were sold to a butcher in Tramore. The payment for these, together with his stipend for his gravedigger or 'verger' duties, comprised the old man's modest income.

Just like my grandfather, The Gusher was 'well in' with the clergy. He had access to the parish priest's library and was permitted to borrow any book he liked. Over a period of years of borrowing the right books, exchanging views with the parish priest and with his greatest friend, my grandfather, The Gusher became quite knowledgeable about literature.

He had a natural penchant for ferreting out

good literature or, as he preferred to put it himself, 'fine writing'. Every time he came to the house he would take me aside with a whispered, 'Come here, Liam, I have something to tell you…' And he would then take me into some wonderful country of the imagination, from which he had just returned.

It was from The Gusher I first heard of Canon Sheehan, the literary parish priest of Doneraile in County Cork, and of the wonderful novels he was writing. The Gusher would often slip me a copy of one of the novels borrowed from our own parish priest's library, with the injunction to 'have it back to me inside a week!' So before I was ten I had read *Lisheen, The Graves at Kilmorna, My New Curate, Luke Delmege* and *The Blindness of Doctor Gray.* When I had read these The Gusher announced that he had a rare treat for me. He would be down to the house very soon and would give it to me then. He duly arrived a few nights later and gave me a small book with a hard, green cover: a book of stories and essays by someone called George Gissing.

I had never heard of Gissing, but The Gusher assured me that after I had read this small book, I would 'crave' some more of Gissing. The old man had a habit of using words that pleased him, like 'crave', as often as he could. He could also be very pedantic about certain things. 'Little things ye pick up if you're close to Fr Donnelly,' he informed me. He stressed to me that the 'G' in Gissing must always be hard; Gissing, never Jissing. I have never doubted this, though over the years I have heard both pronunciations used. Though he had not yet introduced me to Chesterton, of whom he had a very high opinion, he told me that for the fine turn of phrase, there was 'no one to beat Gissing'. As an example he quoted me the opening sentence from one of Gissing's essays: 'Fog from the Channel, with raining scud and the spume of mist rising on the hills, has kept me indoors all day.' Or another fine opening: 'It was twenty years ago, and on an evening in May. I can see the great white clouds that moved across the strip of sky before my window …' The Gusher never tired of quoting something beautiful, something he had just read. I treasure that Gissing book; it is still with me on my desk as I write this. As I look now, seventy years later, at Gissing's book, I pick at random the opening to a story: 'Strong and silent the tide of Thames flowed upward, and over it swept the morning tide of humanity. The dome, the spires, the river frontages slowly unveiled and brightened: there was hope of a fair day.' The Gusher was right when he said: 'Ah, they were all great, Chesterton and Belloc and all that lot. But for the fine phrase, there was no one to turn the fine phrase like Gissing!'

At the beginning of this book, I described the great, reverberating fog-signal of the old Coningbeg Lightship booming out 'like the bellow of a wounded bull'. I like to think that somewhere in the great celestial halls, The Gusher is even now expounding on good writing, citing that line of mine as 'a fine turn of phrase'; perhaps putting it up there beside Gissing! If I am lucky!

14

Most of his time he had worked as a ranchero near El Paso on the Mexican border. His close friend during his years in America had been a very famous writer, Zane Grey.

The third nightly regular to our house was old Tom Mullins. Another contemporary and schoolmate of my grandfather, Tom had spent most of his life in America. Unlike Luke Tarpey, we all knew exactly what Tom Mullins had worked at there. Most of his time there he had worked as a ranchero near El Paso on the Mexican border. I knew this because, from the age of four or five, I remember regular letters coming to my grandfather from his 'friend Tom in the States'. The arrival of these letters at two-month intervals was always treated as a very special occasion. You see, very few people from our parish had emigrated to America, and the few who had were not great letter writers. Indeed, many of them were not even literate. Not so

Tom Mullins, who, according to my grandfather, was well read and had a great command of language. His close friend during his years in America was a very famous writer, Zane Grey. So when Tom's letter arrived, word went out to the far-flung farms across The Glen and The Uplands that Mickey had got the American letter and it would be read at the next Open Night.

Before that reading, my grandfather would sit down with me at the kitchen table and very slowly read the letter to me. I was five years old then and had just started school. Before he started reading he would point out to me the beautiful way in which the script was written, the lovely way in which each separate letter was formed, the special way in which the capital letter at the start of each new sentence was formed with a fine flourish. With capital letters like B, C, D, G, J, O, Q, S and U, he would point out the way in which the following 'small' letter would be enclosed in the loop of the capital letter. I remember asking him where old 'Mexico', as Tom Mullins was known in our community, had learned to write like this. He told me that during the long nights, Mexico would sit on his bed in the bunkhouse of the ranch where he worked and practise writing like that. He said it was called 'calligraphy'. Mexico's friend, Zane Grey, had given him a book about it. Right there at that old kitchen table I decided that was the way I wanted to write. This was a decision that was to cause some tension when I went to school a few months later for the first time.

After reading two or three of these American letters to me, I discovered that my grandfather was quietly practising writing like this himself, so I asked him to teach me also. We would sit together once a week and copy out some of old Mexico's fine script. My grandfather was the best teacher I ever had. He was so good, so easy to learn from, that I feel certain he must have been a teacher in a past incarnation. Within a few weeks I had learned from him how to hold a pen properly and how to swivel it this way and that to get the correct angle to achieve that lovely calligraphic effect. Just recently after my seventy-seventh birthday, I wrote and addressed some letters of thanks for cards I had received. The young lady at the Post Office desk kindly put the stamps on for me and commented, 'Oh, what lovely handwriting!' 'Thank you,' I said, 'My grandfather taught me how to write like that.' She looked a little surprised to hear that someone as old as myself and in a wheelchair could ever have had a grandfather.

The gathering at that next Open Night would be twice the normal size. Tom's letters were listened to avidly as my grandfather read them. They contained very vivid descriptions of the country in which he worked and very often made mention of someone called Zane Grey, a good friend, Tom said. Zane came out to the ranch near El Paso where Tom worked and spent months on end there, researching backgrounds for the stories he was writing. These stories were about 'The West'. He often accompanied Tom on cattle drives and a great friendship was forged between the Irish ranch-hand and the Western writer. During Tom's years at that ranch he received a signed copy of every Zane Grey book published during those years.

So when Tom Mullins returned to spend the rest of his life at home, he had already been nicknamed Mexico by his good friend, my grandfather. Now during his nomadic life in America,

Mexico had certainly gathered no moss, no money and no material possessions. Within a week of returning he was working for a local farmer in The Uplands – Bob Roche – and had accommodation in a loft above the stables. In return he was expected to look after the horses and do just light farm work, leaving him ample time to work around the parish as a chimney-sweep.

My first meeting with Mexico was when he came one July evening to sweep our chimney. He was a small, lean man, his skin wrinkled and bronzed from his days in the southern sun. He always wore a tattered sombrero and a black-and-brown striped poncho. He walked, like my grandfather, with a pronounced limp, though he never used a walking stick. I remember the two of them laughing at having similar handicaps, and being two 'ol' crocks'. I was getting ready to go to boarding school that September, and he questioned me about it. Told me to 'stick with my books and git all the larnin' I could'. Warned me not to end up like him, 'on the scrap heap'.

About this time I was preparing to go to boarding school, thanks to the bounty of my old friend, Luke. The old cow-puncher seemed inordinately pleased. 'Why, boy,' he said, 'this calls for a celebration! Great time in yore life.' He then looked at my grandmother and said, 'Now, Joanna, Michael and myself are goin' to go to the village. Won't be long. Come on Michael!'

He only called my grandfather 'Michael' on very special occasions, so as the two old friends limped off up the road to the village, I wondered what might possibly be in store. 'Expect that pair when ye see them,' my mother said, with a certain doubt. So I waited, wondering what kind of celebration might be coming. They were back within the hour bearing two large bottles of red lemonade (white lemonade had not yet been invented) and assorted packets of biscuits. The big kitchen table was lowered from its place against the wall and the bounty spread on it. Mexico made a little speech. '''Tain't every day a young feller gets the chance to go off to college. Needs to be celebrated! Now that yore off to college, keep yore head down with them thar books. Git all the larnin' ye can. There's more to life than jest travellin'. Ain't that right, Michael?'

'Wouldn't know, Tom,' my grandfather answered, laconically, 'never travelled further than Waterford myself.'

'Don't really make no differ anyways,' Mexico said, tipping his tattered old sombrero over his eyes against the afternoon sun coming through the window. 'Best travel is all in the mind and in books, boy. Don't ye forget books!'

A few days later I returned with my grandfather from footing turf on Annestown bog to find a small brown-paper parcel loosely tied with string on the kitchen table. It was addressed simply to 'The Boy'. It was from Mexico and contained two books with a short note written in his fine calligraphic hand, an exhortation to 'Read 'em, boy! They are fine books, written in great, simple language, and tellin' a great story. Plenty more when you give those back.'

They were two paperbacks in mint condition, *Riders of the Purple Sage* and *Sunset Pass*, both written by his American friend, Zane Grey. The covers of both showed cowboys on beautiful horses; one riding through a canyon and firing from his six-gun at some out-of-picture pursuer, the other another cowboy just riding across the *mesa* in full gallop. The covers of those books provided me with my first sight of what a cowboy looked like. Since then I have been hooked on Zane Grey. Over the years I have managed to build up a little shelf of his books – tattered old paperbacks picked up at jumble sales, at car-boot sales and in dingy little bookshops.

That first time of reading, I read *Riders of the Purple Sage* in four days. I read it with such avidity and total suspension of disbelief that I was lost to everything except the fictional reality of the story. My nights were filled with dreams of gun-battles, cattle-drives and smoke-filled saloons; my days became a wonderfully confused, and confusing, mixture of reality and fantasy. The reality of having to do my chores around the farm, the fantasy of gun-slingers lurking behind every bush and colourful painted ladies twirling parasols, carefully picking their steps along the creaking wooden boardwalks outside saloons. Places with names like The Golden Nugget, The Silver Slipper and Eldorado. The non-stop action, the snappy way the characters spoke to each other, the terse, evocative descriptions of a landscape so wildly beautiful as to be beyond comprehension or belief invaded my youthful senses. At the end of that week I was suffering from glorious, self-inflicted mental and emotional indigestion. I had made a list of words I had never seen before; magical, foreign-sounding words: *mesa, sombrero, gringo, pinto, butte, bandana, peon* – words that sang in my mind and whose meaning I longed to know. With old Mexico's help I soon discovered their meaning.

From that first reading of Zane Grey I was addicted – as surely, as hopelessly as if I had been introduced to some lethal drug. In his fine calligraphic hand, Mexico wrote out a comprehensive glossary of words and phrases for me that further enhanced my reading and inflamed my already fervid imagination. I was, thereafter, able to invest any part of our glen I chose with all the properties of a Zane Grey scenario. Our lean-to hen-house in the haggard would become, in turn, the Bar B cookhouse, the town jail or the Golden Nugget saloon. The rickety old cow-byre standing out in stark relief on the Western skyline made a perfect livery stable, an approaching stagecoach or one of El Paso's many *cantinas*. At a pinch, it could even become a herd of charging buffalo or an Indian raiding party silhouetted against the ever-changing cloud formations behind it.

There was absolutely no limit to the run of my imagination. With imaginary six-gun or rifle, I shot from imaginary horse-back everything that moved around our little farm. Hens and turkeys scattered as I bore down on them at full gallop. I affected an American accent, a drawl similar to that of old Mexico and the characters in *Riders of the Purple Sage*, enraging my long-suffering mother with my incomprehensible slurred mumblings.

'Now, yo must 'scuse me folks!' I would drawl after a hurried tea. 'Must git ma six-guns and mosey on down to the stage office. Thar's a stage a comin' in from El Paso,' I added laconically, as I got a quizzical look from my mother and a broad grin from my father. Grandfather would hide behind his *Cork Examiner* in paroxysms of laughter, while my grandmother quietly read *The Messenger of the Sacred Heart*. Whereupon I would be told quite firmly by my mother, 'Forget about that stage from El Paso and get your homework done.'

On Saturday mornings when I had taken care of my chores and there was no school and homework could be left until Sunday, I would make an announcement quite casually after breakfast. For that was how the cool gunmen in Zane Grey made announcements – very casually.

'Think I'll saddle up the old pinto and ride over the *mesa* to Thunder Butte. Got a tip those desperados who robbed Tuesday's stage are holed up there. Jest might be able to flush 'em out.'

'Don't forget your sombrero,' my father would say, tongue firmly in cheek, while my poor mother just sighed and mumbled something about, 'That Mexico Mullins and his friend, Zane Grey! Bad cess to them!'

I had also, with that unabashed mixture of arrogance and naïvety only possible in the very young teens, begun to write my very own Western novel under the influence of Zane Grey. I filled page after page of two school copybooks with my careful, calligraphic handwriting, in a style that was a direct and unashamed imitation of the great master. It was, I remember, the story of an Irish farm-boy (myself, of course), who emigrates and gets work as a ranch-hand in Arizona. Eventually, after proving himself a hero in many gun-battles, he becomes foreman of the Bar Q ranch, marries the Boss's only daughter and in time becomes owner of the spread.

I called it *The Irish Cowboy* and, though I cannot recall being conscious of this at the time, it was obviously my childish attempt to rearrange Tom Mullins's life and give it a happier ending, not the one he was experiencing as farm-hand and itinerant chimney-sweep. However, that first novel was never finished. The storyline had become inextricably unmanageable and I abandoned it. But, somewhere, I feel sure those two exercise books lie buried in my attic. Dumped under the detritus of the years. I feel equally sure that I will never endeavour to locate them.

Before going away to boarding school that September, at the end of what I will always think of as 'the Summer of Mexico Mullins', I had read three other Zane Grey novels, *Code of the West*, *Nevada* and *To the Last Man*. And old Mexico had talked to me of his life in America. 'An excitin' kinda life,' he admitted, before sadly adding, 'but all you took out of it at the end wus mem'ries.' Still, to this day, I have never met anyone who took so much pleasure in working his way back along the chain of memories, link by inexorable link, as Mexico did.

Two days before I went away to boarding school, I came home in the evening from a day of footing turf on the bog. Mexico had left two books for me. There was a short note with them, again addressed simply to 'The Boy'. 'One book is fer yo to keep, to take to college with yo. The other is jest a lend. When yo finish it yo can have more, whin yo come home for holidays. Good luck, boy … Tom Mullins.'

The book I was intended to keep was a well-worn, well-read copy of *The Imitation of Christ*; the book intended for returning was Zane Gray's *Wild Horse Mesa*. Now during that first term at school, I did read some of *The Imitation*, though it was only after I had read, over and over, *Wild Horse Mesa*. Subsequently, I reached a state of maturity in which I could appreciate that Thomas à Kempis was a more important writer than Grey. But though it does not reflect very well on my character, I had then, and still have, a predilection for the old American teller of tales.

Packing my bags the night before I went away to school, I remember noticing that while the Zane Grey book had been inscribed by the author, 'to my good friend, Tom Mullins, in gratitude, Zane Grey', the older book written by Thomas à Kempis had no such inscription. In my childish naïvety, I asked my grandfather.

'Because,' the old man explained patiently, 'poor old Thomas died about four hundred years ago. Mexico couldn't have known *him*.'

At the end of term, during our four-day Christmas retreat, I became bored with the set spiritual reading, a turgid text called *Where Am I Going?* written by a Jesuit priest whose name I now forget. On the second day of the retreat I removed the loose dust jacket from this book and taped it neatly over *Wild Horse Mesa*. It was a sombre, monochrome jacket – a close-up of a young man with a severe, questioning Jesuitical face onto which was superimposed an outsized bright-red question mark. Very different from the luridly colourful, all-action jacket of *Wild Horse Mesa*, with its Indians in close pursuit of a lone cowboy. Though the Jesuit book jacket was a little smaller than the Zane Grey cover, I thought I had done a good job of camouflage and with arrogant impunity carried it with me to the College Chapel. It gave me a strange, surreptitious thrill to think of all that action going on under the cover of an ostensibly serious text.

After Mass on the third morning of the retreat, in a time set aside for spiritual reading, I was walking in the cloister lost in Zane Grey when a heavy hand on my shoulder jolted me back to reality. Fr Prior, well-practised in such stalking, had been tip-toeing behind me for long enough to know that the book I was reading was not what the jacket proclaimed it to be. The Zane Grey was immediately confiscated and only given back to me on the morning of 12 December when we went home for Christmas.

At home bad news awaited me. In early November Mexico Mullins had died. He had passed away peacefully in his sleep in the loft above the stables at Roche's farm. I was very upset that this idiosyncratic eccentric old man with whom I had talked so seldom and so briefly was gone forever from my life. My grandfather returned the Zane Grey book to Bob Roche, the farmer for whom the old ranchero had worked.

Before returning to school in early January, I visited the old man's grave, as yet unmarked by cross or headstone. I also visited Luke Tarpey's grave on that occasion. By contrast, it was crowned with a very expensive granite headstone, put there by the alcoholic brother who had inherited Luke's share in the farm. I was too young to appreciate the value of the box of

Zane Grey signed first editions left in the loft above the stables at Roche's farm. I just remember feeling sorry that I would now never get to read the other titles. As a young boy brought up in a rural community in a tradition where children were taught to 'know their place', it never occurred to me then to dare ask the people at Roche's farm what had become of old Mexico's books.

When I came home for holidays the following Easter, a small granite headstone had been erected over Mexico's grave. He had left his meagre savings to my grandfather some months before he died to take care of his burial and memorial stone. The simple message on the stone had been composed by Mexico himself at the same time with blanks left for age and dates.

Tom 'Mexico' Mullins
Aged 73 years
Died 11th November 1943
Friend of the writer, Zane Grey

Years later, when I had left The Glen and gone to work in Dublin, I began to think of those first editions and what had become of them. Had they been sold? Given to a museum or library? Not very likely knowing the Roche family for the philistines they were. So on my next visit home, I talked to old Bob's son who had inherited the farm. Yes, he remembered the old trunk under the trestle bed in the loft above the stables. And he remembered that it had been full of books, most of them he said just old paperbacks. Alas, the Roches were not a 'reading' family, so in the general clean-up of the loft, together with other odds-and-ends belonging to Mexico – his threadbare clothes, his poncho, his sombrero – the books had been taken out and burned on a dung heap in the stable yard.

Over the years I have often thought of Tom Mullins, old Mexico. Thought of his wandering life and his lonely end and of the touch of magic and romance he brought to a small boy at a very impressionable age. I still dip into Zane Grey in copies of his books bought in second-hand bookshops during my own wandering life.

I still have the copy of *The Imitation of Christ* which the old man gave me, though I must confess that I haven't read it for many years. The incurable romantic in me still lives on and, sacrilege of sacrileges, I still prefer Zane Grey to Thomas à Kempis. And I often wonder what prompted the old man all those years ago to give me two authors so far removed from each other in time and thought, style and subject matter. Through all his wanderings what prompted Mexico to keep them both in his personal collection? What other incongruous titles lay in that old box under the trestle bed in his Spartan quarters above the stables until they took it out and burned it? I shall never know this side of the grave.

15

Sated and somewhat somnolent after their repast, the diners would enjoy a little time of silence. Then out of that silence would come the voice of one of them telling a story. A ghost story. For that was a good time for a ghost story.

The silent kitchen, the only sounds those of the big clock ticking, the wood crackling on the fire and the crickets chirruping, unseen, in the big hob.

On nights when these three very special visitors came, my mother prepared her very special 'supper'. Large onions in their skins were placed in the red hot ashes round the fire on the hearth. Large potatoes also in their skins were placed beside them. From time to time they were heaped with fresh ashes from the burning wood and turf. After an hour they were taken out and placed in a large wooden dish, ready for serving. Flat wooden plates, knives and forks were then passed round to each diner. On each plate there was a generous dollop of butter – freshly churned 'country butter', lightly salted, gleaming bright yellow in the flickering firelight. The potato skins would have burst, showing the beautifully dry, floury flesh of the potato. The onion skins would have shrivelled, ready to fall off at the first touch. Mugs of fresh buttermilk were then served to slake the thirst of the diners.

Sated and somewhat somnolent after their repast, the diners would enjoy a little time of silence. Then out of that silence would come the voice of one of them telling a story. A ghost story. For that was a good time for a ghost story. The silent kitchen, the only sounds those of the big clock ticking, the wood crackling on the fire and the crickets chirruping, unseen, in the big hob. And on a night when the wind was high and the stars bright, the sound of the wind in the big open chimney. I remember my grandfather holding me as I leaned forward over the fire to look up the chimney and see a piece of dark-blue night sky and a little cluster of sparkling stars framed in the rectangle at the top. When he had set me back safely beside him in the inglenook, he would tell me why the stars were so bright on windy nights. On windy nights, he said, the high wind washing over the stars polished them till they shone brightly and danced. I believed the old man then, and I still believe him whenever I stand under the open night sky and listen to the great wash of wind overhead and see the bright stars sparkle and dance.

In this wonderful atmosphere, so conducive to quiet storytelling, my febrile mind would hang on every word and I would, reluctantly, be sent off to bed after the first story was told. That first story was always a story of 'Kitty the Hare' read by my grandfather from the latest issue of *Ireland's Own*. These were very popular ghost stories written by Victor O'D. Power. They were a bit eerie, but suitable for children.

Afterwards, lying in bed, I could hear the gentle drone of the voice of the story teller echoing from the silence of the big kitchen as I drifted into sleep. There would be no loud music, no singing, no dancing on nights like this; only the occasional sound of a very gentle slow air from Luke Tarpey's fiddle. The tune played very low under the voice of the teller of the tale, a sound to accentuate the sadness and eeriness of the story. On one occasion, determined to hear fully one of the 'real ghost stories', I managed to hide in the kitchen instead of going to bed. I hid behind two big water buckets, covered over with gauze. I only did that once, and for two good reasons: the great risk of being caught out of bed, and the story I heard was too scary.

Old Luke Tarpey told it in the quiet, gentle way that only he knew how. The location was very near our house: a steep hill on the road to Tramore. There had once been a quarry there, and over fifty years before, in the course of blasting the rock, a workman had been killed by some flying splinters of sharp stone. Ever since then, travellers coming along this road from Tramore had seen the ghost of this unfortunate man blocking the road before them as they came up the hill. It was a steep hill and cyclists would always dismount and walk up. People in a pony-drawn trap or a horse-drawn trap or cart would always urge the animal to a brisk trot up the hill. But, always, however the traveller approached the top of the incline – on foot and rolling the bicycle, in the relative safety of the trap or aboard the cart – the apparition of the quarryman would inevitably await them at the summit.

At first, nearing the top, there would be this sensation of a very cold draught of foul air, like stagnant water, blowing down the road from the top of the hill. Before anything was ever seen, ponies or horses would grow very restless, whinnying loudly and stomping their hooves, pawing the ground and refusing to go on. Their drivers would then get down from the trap or cart and endeavour to lead the frightened animal past the top of the hill. Some animals, less skittish and frightened than others, would reluctantly allow themselves to be led past the apparition of the quarryman standing in the middle of the road. This was quite horrific. When the poor man had been killed his face and head had taken the brunt of the explosion; where the face had been nothing remained now but a mass of red pulp. Anyone who dared pass this fearsome sight had to walk right through the apparition, which stood over six feet tall in the middle of the narrow road. Some brave souls had walked through with their bicycles; others had led their frightened, whinnying horses and ponies through. No one had ever been harmed, just frightened. Several men had been so frightened that they went back down the hill and took a four-mile detour to get home.

I was not discovered hiding behind the water buckets listening to the story. I crept off to my bed and covered my face in the bedclothes. I could not sleep that night. I kept seeing the blood-covered face of the quarryman standing over me.

16

> *Almost every story he read to me had some reference to history so every story became also a history lesson. My first school was there at that open hearth, my first teacher was old Mickey the caffler and my first lessons were in country lore, history and the literature of many countries.*

Sometimes I take down my battered, faded-brown, old copy of Longfellow's poems. The cover has long since been lost in my many changes of domicile. I read again, the ghost of my grandfather at my shoulder, correcting as he did over seventy years ago my mispronunciation of the magical Indian names in the 'Song of Hiawatha'. Names he was taught how to pronounce by the old parish priest who gave him the book.

I also remember with great joy the lovely set of Walter Scott's *Waverly Novels* on that shelf beside the Welsh Dresser. *Heart of Midlothian, Ivanhoe, Kenilworth*… All read to me by that wonderful old man, snug in the inglenook, when the winter wind wailed in the big open chimney and unseen crickets sang beneath the red-hot hob. I remember also two large volumes of *Collected Essays* of Robert Louis Stevenson and G. K. Chesterton. The combination of the heat from the big open fire and the gentle rhythm of my grandfather's reading sometimes sent me to sleep.

The old man had the great gift of knowing instinctively when I was lost for the meaning of certain words or phrases. He would stop reading and with great patience explain whatever I didn't understand. And almost every story he read to me had some reference to history, so every story became also a history lesson. My first school was there at that open hearth, my first teacher was old Mickey the Caffler and my first lessons were in country lore, history and the literature of many countries, learned to the background of cricket song.

My grandfather never saw himself as a farmer, even as a small farmer. He was just a man who'd been blessed with a little bit of good land, and that was that. He never considered himself lucky when anything good befell him; he always saw himself as blessed. If he achieved anything, he was never proud of his achievement – just glad and in a celebratory mood, which he insisted on sharing with his neighbours.

One of the things I remember with most pleasure from my childhood is the wonderful way in which the 'barter' system and the system of neighbour helping neighbour worked. From the age of seven, not a week went by when I wasn't involved. After school or at weekends I would tackle up our donkey and cart and load some sides of home-cured bacon for neighbours across The Glen. My grandfather had a reputation as being 'a great man to kill a pig and cure it'. For weeks on end there would be sides of bacon and pigs' heads, well salted, hanging on a pulley high up in our big chimney. While they were being 'smoked', only wood was used on the fire, a slow-burning green ash whose smoke was most astringent but gave a fantastic flavour to the meat hanging in our chimney. After four or five weeks of 'smoking' the meat would be taken down and put to steep in a tub of pure spring water. When the steeping process was over the meat was then rubbed all over with sea salt and left to settle for a couple of days before a gentle washing. It was then ready to cook.

These trips across The Glen, and sometimes to The Uplands, were undertaken on the barter basis. I would always return with a couple of newly slaughtered lambs or some cuts of beef. A leg of lamb or a few choice cuts of beef would then be bartered at the village shop for whatever groceries we had drawn down against them. My grandfather and myself fished twice a week, depending on the weather. We fished from his fourteen-foot sailing boat, and I will never forget those days spent bobbing about on the great sea. Very often we would go far inshore, right under our forbidding black cliffs, for that was where certain fish ran. I would take the catch when we came home and place three or four different types of fish in wooden boxes. These were laid out on the little donkey cart, and I would set out across the dusty roads of two parishes to sell the catch – mackerel, whiting, pollock, gurnet and occasionally a few flounders. The 'fish money' always went into a special clothing fund, spent when my mother and father went to Waterford City twice a year to buy clothes for the whole family.

In all of these barter transactions, there was never a quibble, never an argument, no pound-for-pound comparisons. And it was the same with days given to a neighbour to save hay or cut turf. All of this was never done on a quid pro quo basis. We were there when they needed us, and they were there when we needed them. There was never a question of owing a day or being owed a day *in lieu*. Everything was done with a great generosity of spirit as need demanded.

17

For over a hundred years, generations of my family had been born, lived their lives and died in this old long-house — the sea had become part of the rhythm of our lives, coursing in our veins like some salt-red blood.

My maternal grandmother was a very reserved little lady. She had been a priest's housekeeper from the time she left school, aged about fourteen or fifteen, until she married and came to live in the long-house near the sea. For over one hundred years, generations of my family had been born and lived out their lives in this old house. One of the two great omnipresences in their lives was the incessant sound of the sea. Long before we became conscious of it, the sea had become part of the rhythm of our lives, coursing in our veins like some salt-red blood.

As was destined for me, successive generations of my forebears had been awakened by the sound of the sea. They had fallen asleep or in bad weather been kept from sleep by the roar of the sea. Here on this remote, black-cliffed coast facing westward into the roiling Atlantic, more than sun, moon, stars or mechanical timepiece, the sea had dictated the rhythm of their days and nights like some hypnotic metronome. For the sea incessantly languidly lapped or pitilessly pounded these immemorial cliffs, whispering or booming as veering wind and cyclic tide dictated.

The other great omnipresence in The Glen was the ringing of the Angelus bell, twice every day, at noon and at six in the evening. The mellow old metal rang out with nearly as many variations as the sound of the sea. Depending on where the wind stood, it was heard clearly or muffled. In heavy rain its tone was dull; in dry weather it sounded crisp and clear. But whatever its tone it was as much a part of life in the parish as was the sound of the sea. Parishioners in The Glen and The Uplands set their watches and clocks by it and stood, wherever they happened to be, in respectful silence as they recited the Angelus.

I was nine when my grandmother died so I have many lovely memories of her. She dressed all in black, and on Sundays she wore a beautiful, black crocheted shawl, which she had made herself, when going to Mass. Very refined and lady-like, she pretended to be utterly outraged at some of my grandfather's utterances. I don't think she was in the least outraged, just a bit shocked at his outspokenness. For instance if he had been to the village, she would always ask him if he had met anyone on his journey. He would sometimes answer, 'Yes, Joanna, I met that one of the Paddy Lar Powers and there's a hell of a lot of her split.' This meant Nellie Lar, a very tall girl with very long legs. My grandmother would hide her face in her shawl with a great sigh and say, 'You're a terrible man Mickey Kiely!' I always felt she was laughing behind the cover of the shawl. One thing I was always sure of: she loved my grand-father more than anyone or anything in this life, and he loved her in return.

I can remember her from the time I first started to walk. She was still able to get up every day and sit beside the fire and chat and be part of the life we enjoyed in that big, flagged kitchen. My mother would mix the ingredients for some of the lovely sweet cakes she baked in the big griddle over the open fire. Granny would help her and she would always leave a little of the mixture on the side of the bowl for me. I loved to run my fingers round the bowl and then lick and suck them. When mother saw what I was doing she would chase me away from the table, indignant at my lack of manners.

18

Rhododendron bushes with huge pale blue, white and pink flowers overhung the seat. Wild flowers bloomed all round us in the grass. A choir of birds sang, unseen, in the surrounding bushes. And behind the seat the stream gurgled by, making its own very special water music.

Even as a child I could clearly see the love of these old people for each other. They were always concerned for each other's ailments. My grandmother suffered, as did most old people then, from bad arthritis. At that time, there was little choice of pain relief. But my grandfather never stopped looking for something to ease her pain. And she never stopped worrying about his 'bad leg'. Every so often my grandfather would hear of some herbalist or faith healer, maybe ten miles away in another parish. He would be off in the donkey-trap, or on his 'one-legged bicycle', as he called it, to investigate the situation and ascertain if there was any hope of some relief for his wife in what they had to offer. And there was always the hope that it might work too for 'the pain in his bad leg'. Whenever he went in the donkey-trap, The Gusher went with him. They both loved a day away in what they called 'the far country', the mountainy land in the foothills of the Comeraghs.

Out of these 'reconnaissance trips', as my grandfather called them, there sometimes came what promised to be relief for my grandmother's rheumatic pain. Then after weeks of assiduously trying out diverse pills, potions and poultices, the old couple would come to the conclusion that 'nothing worked'. My grandfather's search would go on relentlessly. He had loved this little lady all his adult life and would continue to do so for the remainder of his life, and after.

Nowhere was this love manifested more than in the way he indulged my grandmother's great love of flowers. Traditionally there had been very little flower-growing in rural communities. Perhaps some farmer's wife who had enjoyed a boarding-school education and the inevitable course in Domestic Science 'with the nuns' would make a token effort in cultivating some flowers. A small bamboo stand somewhere inside the house, in the window recess of a parlour or inside a porch would accommodate a collection of geranium plants. If the window ledges of the house were suitable, indoors or outdoors, perhaps a few window boxes, with an assortment of small blooms. From being in other houses in The Glen, I so well remember my grandmother talking about the unpleasant smell of geraniums, especially indoors, and the way they shed their leaves in great abundance at certain times. With a great good-natured laugh, my grandfather would say to my grandmother, 'Oh, that may all be true, Joanna, but there's another reason I wouldn't inflict geraniums on anybody I loved!' Yet, he would never tell her what the other reason was.

There were things, some very 'risky' things, he would say in front of my grandmother, and just some few things he wouldn't ever say in her presence. The rest of us in the house knew the reason in the case of the geraniums. In some remote houses, at the top end of The Glen, certain people were known to use the geranium pots as 'piss pots', to quote my grandfather. These pots were kept under the beds at night. My grandfather also said that the more polite denizens of The Glen and The Uplands used the more polite name for such pots. They referred to them as '*gerry* pots'. Like many of the stories my grandfather told, their attraction was in never being sure whether he was telling the truth or, as he would often say of someone else, 'chancing his *arm* with his *tongue* in his *cheek*'.

However, the old man would never settle for skimpy window boxes or bedraggled, smelly geraniums when it came to flowers for *his* Joanna. My mother remembered, as a child of six or seven, helping him put down the rose bushes along the whole length of our house. She remembered each separate bush being placed in the narrow bed against the front wall, the care with which each one was planted in the well-manured earth – each one of the fourteen equidistant from the last. Over the years, as they grew, any weakling was instantly replaced by a new bush to make sure they all grew to a uniform height.

My mother also remembered being asked to stand against the roses to measure their rate of growth. One spring when she was in her late teens and had stopped growing, she remembered my grandfather's great joy at discovering that the rose bushes had outstripped her in height. There would be no need for the measuring process to go on anymore. From then on it was a matter of careful husbandry – mulching, pruning, spraying against the dreaded greenfly and constantly checking that the staples holding each branch against the wall were secure. Until the time the old man could no longer walk and was hospitalised, this regime of loving care was religiously observed. Even after my grandmother died, for many years the roses were tended. Nothing was ever actually said, but we all knew that for grandfather, 'Joanna's roses' would always live in his heart and in his mind. They would always be tended with the same loving impulse that drove him to plant them for her so many years before.

It was this same loving impulse that drove him to transmogrify what was an old, ramshackle haggard directly behind our house into a country garden of stupendous beauty. My mother was in her teens at the time and remembers my grandfather walking round the old haggard for an hour or more one spring morning. My grandmother and herself watched him from the kitchen window. Watched him pacing between the old abandoned remains of hay-ricks and straw-ricks, pushing bushes to one side, measuring distances from one point to another with outstretched arms and blackthorn walking-stick and muttering to himself. They were nonplussed at this behaviour, as he had said nothing about the haggard to them. When he came in they asked him what he was doing out there with all that measuring and talking to himself. He just smiled his enigmatic smile and assured them it was only a little 'reconnaissance job'. This just left them more puzzled than ever.

That evening, after supper and Rosary, the purpose of the 'reconnaissance' was revealed. He sat down at the big table, lit the oil-lamp, took out his big notepad and pencil and started to draw. After a while he called my grandmother, my father, my mother and my uncle Tim, who was then twelve, to join him at the table. He had sketched a rough plan for the haggard. It was to be cleared of all the old rubble and turned into a country garden. A garden for my grandmother. A garden for Joanna. He had the whole shape of the garden in his mind, he just wanted to know what flowers she would like there. Not roses. She had plenty of roses on the front of the house.

Anything but roses. So began, my mother remembered, what was to be a long process in the making of 'the garden'. Eventually, after almost two years of hard work, clearing all trace of the old ricks, cutting away all the dense, tangled undergrowth, making the little paths that zigzagged between and round the flower beds, 'Joanna's Garden' became a reality.

On my grandmother's suggestion, the choice of flowers and shrubs should be left to my father. He was the one who had trained as a bothyman. So from the start the garden had a profusion of daffodils, primroses, bluebells, pampas grass and large bushes of rhododendron and fuchsia planted round the perimeter. Very late in the laying out of the garden, my grandmother decided she would love to have 'just a few beehives'. She had always wanted to have her own honey. So, four hives were put in place, in a quiet, out-of-the-way corner, which could not be easily accessed by young children. By the time I first remember seeing it, when I was three or four, the haggard had been maturing for long enough to be an enchanted place. A place that had been lovingly looked after by two men – my father and grandfather – men who loved their work and also loved the old lady for whom the garden had been created.

Incredibly, despite the total transmogrification of the dilapidated old haggard, it continued to be called the haggard, never the garden. When I was six or seven, I remember my grandmother coming out to 'sit in the haggard' on fine days. My mother would help her walk out to a very special seat my father had made for her, set in a beautiful corner beside the stream. Rhododendron bushes, with huge pale blue, white and pink flowers overhung the seat; wildflowers bloomed all round us in the grass. A choir of birds sang, unseen, in the surrounding bushes. And just behind the seat the stream gurgled by, making its own very special water music. The little old lady, all dressed in black, would sit and wait patiently for Mickey to come out and read us a story. Eventually he would come and read us some wonderful historical tale from *Ireland's Own*. Afterwards they would chat, and my grandmother would remind him of the story of Bob Pats Power and the mad bull, and he would tell us that story, adding, she said, a few little things that weren't in it the last time of telling. He would just laugh and remind her that that was the way of all good storytelling – adding a few legs that weren't there before.

My grandmother died when I was nine. She died in July, in a very warm summer. The day before her death she and I sat on the old garden seat. She wasn't feeling too well and didn't want any stories told. She just wanted Mickey to come and sit with us, maybe have a little chat and listen to the sounds of the haggard. The rhododendrons were in full bloom: great, round balls of wonderful colour. A gentle wind was stirring the leaves. As the two of us sat and waited, one large bloom somehow became detached from the tree and fell with a gentle splash into the stream. We watched as it swirled in the current and then began to move away. My grandmother watched it go, commenting on how like a little pink-sailed boat it was. She wondered where it would end up. Would it get as far as the sea? Or would it get stuck somewhere on its journey, stuck in one of the snags of driftwood along the way? She looked sad as the pink rhododendron boat slipped round a bend in the stream and was gone. Just then my grandfather came, and for a great surprise, brought his fiddle with him. He was a good fiddle player, but rarely played as he preferred to tell stories. However, on this occasion, he had been looking out from the kitchen window at the two of us and thought we looked a bit down. So what better way to cheer us than with a bit of sad music.

He sat down between us and, instinctively knowing what my grandmother liked, he began to play 'Fanny Poer'. I looked at her as he finished and saw that she was crying. The old man put the fiddle aside, took her hand and said just one word, 'Joanna.' But he put all the feeling, meaning and love of which he was capable into that one word. She looked at him, her face all tear-stained, and said, 'Mickey, I think it's time to go in.' So, she walking between us, we went in. She left her haggard for the last time. She died peacefully in her sleep, that night. My grandfather, having some premonition, had sat beside the bed all night. He said he knew when she had passed away: the room felt suddenly cold and very empty. Just as I imagine his life was ever after.

I was an altar boy in the parish church at that time and I remember being greatly moved by the tributes paid to my grandmother at her funeral. For the first time then, at the age of nine, I was suddenly aware of how tremendously blessed I was to belong to a family where love and caring were the most important things in life. My grandfather lived on for seven years after her death, and all that time, with my father's help, he was meticulous in his tending to the 'haggard garden'. The garden he had created out of love for his young wife so many years ago.

19

From the start, family and friends, fair-minded though they were, had doubted the wisdom of young Margaret Kiely taking her new husband to live in The Glen. To them, he was a 'Dublin Jackeen'. And how he would hit it off with old Mickey the caffler was a moot point.

My father, Henry Long, was born in Dublin. In 1922, when he was fifteen, he came to Waterford with his whole family. His father, William (Bill) Long, was what was known in those days as a 'bothy-man'; nowadays he would be called a gardener. Born in York and a Protestant, he worked for over ten years as head bothy-man to the Viceroy in Phoenix Park. This job included the perk of living in a very beautiful old lodge at the Chapelizod Gate of Phoenix Park. Here, my father and his siblings, two brothers and two sisters were born.

My grandmother Long was a Catholic, a Kavanagh from Wicklow. In accordance with

Catholic Church law of that time, children of a mixed marriage had to be brought up as Catholics. From the formation of the new state, warning bells were ringing, loud and clear, for any Protestant Englishmen who were employed by British masters. Henceforth would be emerging the men with 'national records'. They would be the ones accommodated with jobs and the perks of living in lodges. At more than one level the old order was changing and giving place to the new.

So my paternal grandfather, grandmother and their five children moved to Waterford. The English Protestant bothy-man, unwanted now by the new state, found himself a job with Power's Nurseries. He became senior bothy-man there. Within the year he had employed his son, Henry, as a trainee bothy-man. While still a trainee, my father met my mother, Mary Kiely, then a waitress in O'Brien's Tea Rooms in Tramore. After a three-year courtship, they were married and came to make their home in the old long-house in The Glen, where my grandparents lived alone.

From the start, family and friends, fair-minded though they were, doubted the wisdom of young Mary Kiely taking her new husband to live in The Glen. To them he was a 'Dublin Jackeen', and how he would hit it off with old Mickey the Caffler was a moot point. They need not have worried. The old countryman and the Dublin Jackeen, however incongruous they looked together, were instantly compatible. They shared the same sense of humour and respected the same things: women, children, their neighbours, nature and animals. Their opinions diverged somewhat on religion, and politics, but they were both intelligent enough to realise that religion and politics were, as my grandfather put it, 'dangerous ground'. A bit, he opined, like bogholes in the marsh to the north of the house, where good men had gone in and never come out. So there was a tacit agreement that religion and politics were not up for discussion.

There was, however, a subject which engaged them both from the start: the few acres of good land at the back of the house and to what use it could best be put. My grandfather had always been satisfied to grow enough basic vegetables for ourselves: potatoes, cabbage, turnips and carrots. My father had other ideas, which he carefully outlined to the older man. We were only three miles from Tramore, and Tramore had three big hotels and five or six smaller ones. They were all booked out for the summer season. Between them they served hundreds of meals every day and used a lot of vegetables. Not just the basic ones my grandfather grew, but many others, such as lettuce, beetroot, cauliflower, tomatoes, runner beans. And where did they buy these? From two wholesale greengrocers in the town; paying top price for them, as the greengrocers had to have their margin.

Before my first birthday my grandfather and his new son-in-law had finalised plans to cultivate an acre of good ground beside the river as a market garden. My father undertook to talk to all the major hotels in Tramore, establishing what produce they might buy. My grandfather took responsibility for the preparation of the river field. After my father had ascertained that the hotels would definitely buy certain vegetables and fruit, my grandfather proceeded to have the river field tilled. This was done on the barter system. Neighbours came with horse and plough and harrow. Seed was purchased from the meagre personal savings of my father and grandfather, helped by some credit from a seed merchant in Tramore. At that time, the early 1940s, banks had no place in the lives of country folk like us. Loans were not in existence and business was transacted on the basis of mutual trust and the goodwill of neighbours. The modest venture prospered.

During the summer holidays from school, I would go three times a week, my donkey-cart laden with fruit and vegetables, to deliver to the various hotels in Tramore. I loved this job. I would leave home very early in the morning and make my first delivery to The Grand Hotel, the biggest of all the hotels in town. Here the head porter was very kind to me and would always instruct one of his trainees to unload the boxes. He would take me to the enormous kitchen and treat me to a 'Royal breakfast', as he put it. Fresh orange juice, bacon, egg, black and white pudding, a slice of liver and tea and toast and marmalade. My last call would be to The Majestic Hotel, another top place. Here I would always be just in time for lunch.

Seven other families inhabited The Glen, small-holders like ourselves making a living from the little fertile fields and the sea. This, then, was the milieu into which I was born. A remote country parish, where outside The Glen, your nearest neighbour was two miles away on The Uplands. Our parish was a place of simple folk. Money was not a currency in everyday use. It was used only to pay the twice-yearly taxes and for an annual shopping trip to Waterford City, ten miles away, to purchase necessary clothes. It was from this meagre amount that the money was taken to fund the market-garden project. Neighbour trusted neighbour and the barter system worked well. We were a humble, self-reliant community and the architects of our own un-ambitious, simple destinies.

Pride, greed and envy had no place in our lives. Our occasional, almost accidental, modest achievements merely cause for mutual, thankful celebration. Everything was shared and there was joy and great contentment in the sharing.

20

I remember very vividly two things that struck me forcibly on that first visit: how small the kitchen was compared to our big country kitchen and how large the back garden was. I think I was surprised that a house so close to the city centre should have any garden at all.

I must have been seven or eight when I paid my first visit to my paternal grandparents at their home in Waterford City. They lived on a long hill road not far from the centre in a small, two-storey, red-brick terrace house with no front garden. I remember very vividly two things that struck me forcibly on that first visit: how small the kitchen was compared to our big country kitchen and how large the back garden was. I think I was surprised that a house so close to the city centre should have any garden at all. The garden was very long, but narrow. It was so neat and tidy and generally well-kept with more than half of it taken up with very neat drills and beds of vegetables. There was a section with some beautiful fruit bushes and at the back there was a colourful bank of flowers.

I could not help wondering at how black the soil was. I remember asking my father on our way back home about the colour of the soil. He said it was due to the careful use of good fertilisers and being kept free of weeds. Grandad Long, he explained, had been a gardener all his working life and loved gardens and all the wonderful things you could grow in them. Now that he had retired he was able to give all his time to his own garden. I then had to ask my father what retirement was. I had never, up to then, heard the word. Very patiently he explained what retirement meant. Then, anticipating my next question, he went on to explain that people seldom retired in the country. They all worked for themselves and went on working for as long as their health allowed them, unlike people like Grandad Long, who worked for someone else and had to retire when they came to a certain age. Aged eight, I didn't really understand but thought it best to just shrug my shoulders and say, 'Oh, I see.' But I didn't, not really, not just then.

After that I visited Grandad and Granny Long several times, sometimes with my father, sometimes with my mother and sometimes with both. I always enjoyed spending time in the garden with Grandad, having him tell me about the different vegetables growing there. And walking between the fruit bushes, I was allowed to sample some of the ripening fruit. Granny Long would always tap on the kitchen window and shout to Grandad, 'Bill, too much of that fruit will make the boy sick!' Whereupon Grandad would wink at me and, unseen, slip me a fistful of plump, ripe berries.

At first Grandad frightened me a bit. He was so tall, over six feet, with big, broad shoulders. He had the biggest moustache I had ever seen, waxed and curled up at the ends. And his eyes looked so bright they might be getting ready to pop out of his head. His voice was loud, deep and sounded a bit grumpy. Worst of all, he had an English accent. Attuned as my young ears were to Irish country accents, I found it impossible to understand some of what he was saying to me. In fairness to him, however, he seemed to sense this and began to speak more slowly and simply, in order that I might better know what he was saying. After a couple of visits I began to see him as a kindly old man and grew less fearful of him as time went by.

Granny Long was a large Wicklow woman who wore a wrap-around pinafore apron and was always working around the kitchen. Even as she talked to you, she was busy washing dishes, scrubbing worktops, preparing meals. She never seemed to sit down, read a book or a newspaper or listen to the wireless. On the other hand, Grandad had his certain times of day when he sat in a big, old easy-chair in a corner of the kitchen, smoking his big, bent-shank pipe, reading a book or just listening to the wireless. Granny never seemed to resent this, just proceeded to sweep, dust or continue doing whatever she happened to be doing. She would then bring him a mug of tea and some biscuits. I was fascinated by his special mug, which had a little lip with a cut-away centre inside the rim. This prevented his moustache from dipping into the tea.

One day, when my father and I arrived, Grandad was not there. Granny said he would be back soon. Just then there was knock on the door and I heard Granny say from the little hallway, 'Oh, Fr Rattigan! Come in, come in.' She then ushered in Fr Rattigan and introduced us. He was her parish priest. Shortly after that Grandad arrived home. On seeing the priest there, he froze. When he spoke his voice was deep and tremulous, his eyes popping from their sockets. 'Reverend, you are not welcome in this house. Now, please leave!' My father, embarrassed, tried to intervene but was brusquely told, 'Henry! Stay out of this.'

My father said nothing, neither did poor Granny Long and the priest left. The four of us sat in silence for what seemed an eternity. Grandad, having regained his equilibrium, stood up and putting his hand on my shoulder suggested we go and see how the fruit was coming along in the garden. Reluctantly I went out with him. I picked and ate the fruit without relish. I never enjoyed visiting the house again. Somehow, without understanding it fully then, I felt I had been close to something very wrong and very ugly, which my father called 'religious intolerance' when he explained it to me later. But whatever one called it, my initial feeling about it had been correct.

After that incident our visits grew less frequent and less enjoyable. The love between my

maternal grandparents was palpable, their closeness something beautiful and all enveloping. In
their presence you felt safe. With my paternal
grandparents that climate of love, caring and
closeness was missing. There was a certain in-
ternecine threat hanging over the little house.
You couldn't feel safe there anymore.

About a year after that we received a telegram
to say that Grandad Long had been admitted to
hospital, having suffered a severe heart attack at
home. My father, mother and I went to the hospital. The old man had recovered somewhat
from that first attack. He sat in bed, propped by
pillows, looking deathly pale. His eyes had lost
their fierceness and their lustre, his cheeks were
sunken and his skin pallid. His great moustache,
the ends unwaxed, looked unkempt and ugly
about his mouth. Granny Long sat by the bed,
numbed by what had happened. Though I was
only nine years old I had some understanding of
the kind of life they must have had, labouring in
this very mixed marriage. I was full of empathy
for them both. My uncle Willie, my father's
brother, was at the bedside later when the old
man suffered another heart attack. This attack

took him in a brief, severe convulsion of pain and he passed over into another life. He was buried in the Protestant cemetery just round the corner from the house in which he'd lived.

After that my father and I visited Granny Long regularly. We enjoyed some good times with her, and my father kept the garden in good shape. About six months after old Bill's death, she was diagnosed as having cancer of the liver. Despite surgery and subsequent treatment, she passed away before the end of the year in which her husband had died. She was buried in one of the many Catholic cemeteries on the other side of the city.

I sometimes think of how terrible that condition regarding the children's religious upbringing was for couples in a mixed marriage. As with Granny and Grandad Long, it created a rift from the time the first child was born. Endless arguments about education, church-going and so many things that should have been bonding proved instead to be sundering. I remember just before I went to boarding school my father talking to me about religion and how great it was that we were all Catholics and had none of the awful rows about religion that he remembered from his childhood. He told me then that, up to the time he met my mother, he had been a very, very lukewarm Catholic. Since the time they decided to get married he had tried to be more serious about the practice of his religion. He had reached some kind of plateau, where he felt happy about religion for the first time in his life.

21

*Then came the 'candle treatment'.
I would take several large, white wax
candles. With a big knife, lifted without
her knowledge from my mother's kitchen,
I would shave the candles very finely
onto the wooden platform. This would
create, after the first dancers had
'tested' it, a fine, easy, but not slippery,
surface on which to dance for the night.*

At the back of our house, where the three roads met, there was a lovely, grassy triangle. From Saint Patrick's Day until mid-September, this triangle was used to accommodate a triangular dance floor. There was a dance every Sunday night and sometimes on special nights during the week: a church holiday, an anniversary or the night of a local wedding. The triangular, wooden dance floor was made up of five sections, and these sections were stored between dances in the back of our old barn. From the time I was nine, these sections were my responsibility, for which

I was paid five shillings every dance night by the Dance Committee.

The five sections were too big for me to carry, but my father agreed to do this for me. For the first week he joked about taking two shillings of my five for this service. Eventually he told me he was only joking. My work really started when the pieces were in place on the level green patch, slotted together in a special way to prevent them from parting when the dancing started. Then came the 'candle treatment'. I would take several large, white candles. With a big knife, lifted without permission from my mother's kitchen, I would shave the candles very finely onto the wooden platform. This would create, after the first dancers had 'tested' it, a fine, easy, but not slippery, surface on which to dance. Though, sometimes, if there was a big crowd and lots of dancers on the floor, it might need more of the 'candle treatment' before the end of the night. Very often it would be getting late, past my bedtime, when this repeat treatment was needed, and my father would do the job for me.

A full orchestra of musicians would assemble half an hour before the dancing was due to commence. This orchestra was made up mostly of players who played at the Open Nights in our kitchen. Fiddlers, banjo players, box players, bodhran players, concertina players, mouth-organ players and sean-nós singers would take their places on one side of the triangle. The other two sides were for the audience. Plain wooden seats with no back-rests lined the three sides. The two sides not used by the orchestra were reserved for the elderly folk who couldn't stand or sit around on the grass. These were mostly ladies, for whom the platform dance was the highlight of the week. A group or two of staid old men would stand on the periphery, smoking their pipes or chewing tobacco and spitting the horrible, brown-coloured juice all over the lovely shining leaves of my grandmother's rhododendrons. Others, younger spectators would sit around on the grass or stand in little groups against the parapet of the bridge between the dances. One or two of the elderly ladies, stirred by the music, would occasionally leave their seats at the invitation of some gallant young man to slide their way through a slow waltz.

These elderly ladies seated on the backless forms were our targets. When the dance was well started, my school friends and I would steal

163

down under the bridge and fill a couple of old sacks with frogs. The commotion the big fat bull-frogs made on being captured went totally unnoticed, lost in the greater commotion of the furious music and the dancers swirling on the dance floor. The frogs would plop, all ooze and sticky mess, one atop the other into our sacks. Quietly we would drag the sacks across the grass and place them behind the two rows of seats occupied by the old ladies and perhaps a few old men. We would then wait; timing was all-important now. At the end of a set, just when the music had died and the dancers were shuffling off the floor, we would open the mouths of the sacks and spill out an avalanche of slimy, gurgling frogs right under the seats. The old ladies, feeling the slimy movement around their feet and ankles, would begin to scream. The screaming would last for as long as the frogs slid around under the seats. In an effort to drown it out the orchestra would strike up its loudest music. This only exacerbated the cacophony of sound and resulted in total bedlam. The confusion could only be assuaged by 'Snooks' Hayes, cloth cap askew with the front to back, leaping onto the platform, his mouth organ ringing out 'Planxty Green'.

Nobody suspected my school friends and myself. We found it difficult to suppress the laughter when we listened to some of the reasons put forward for this 'plague of frogs', as it was called. The reason that tickled our fancy most was that the frogs had been upset by the loud music and had tried to attack the area from which it came. Eventually, one of us was careless in concealing a sack and it was found under the bridge. This caused some fresh thinking. We realised that having had our harmless fun for so long the time had come to stop. I don't think anyone ever suspected us. If they had, we'd have known all about it.

Thereafter, when my time came for bed on these 'platform nights', I would lie awake for a long time just listening to the music, the singing and the rhythm of the dancing feet. That was when I first came to appreciate the very special sound of such music played in the open air. I would drift into sleep, on these magic nights and dream of . . . frogs!

22

My grandfather's great idea turned out to be just that – a great idea! Right then we would sit down, and find names for all six cats, from the lovely placenames in my new atlas.

From the time I could creep around on all fours, I remember there were always cats and dogs about our kitchen. Creeping across the floor I would come quite literally face to face with one of the two dogs or one of the six cats. The dogs had names – Fin and Butcher. The cats had no names. This didn't bother me while I was down there at their level and had no real knowledge of names anyway. But as I got older and began to understand the reason for having names, I began to wonder why our two dogs had names, but our six cats did not. When I was about three and a half, I managed to convey my concern to my grandfather. Though he didn't seem to share my concern, he did admit to thinking it unfair that the cats should be nameless. He would, thereafter, with a laugh often refer to the fact that he had seen 'one of the nameless ones' around the haggard, sniffing at the beehives. We must, he stated solemnly, find names for every cat as soon as we could. But 'soon as we could' turned out to be a very long time. By then I was seven and had just got my first school atlas. This was the most colourful book I had ever seen, full of maps of every country in the world, in a multitude of bright colours – reds, blues, greens, yellows – and names of places that sounded like poetry.

On the evening of the day I first got this atlas, I showed it to my grandfather. I was sitting at the kitchen table doing my homework. He stood behind me as I turned the pages. He was silent for a long while. Then he put a hand on my shoulder, announcing that he had a great idea and we would talk about it after tea.

His great idea turned out to be just that – a great idea! Right then we would sit down, and find names for all six cats from the lovely place-names in the atlas. An hour later we had decided on the names – Moscow, Oslo, Porto, Florence, Venice and Paris. He insisted that we sat there for fifteen minutes and repeated the names to each other, over and over again. He wanted to be sure they sounded right and that we were happy with them.

Next day came the difficult part. Outside, watching all six as they drank from the big dish of milk, we tried to fit a name to each cat. Grandfather thought the names Porto, Florence, Oslo and Venice should be given to the four female cats, and the names Moscow and Paris to the two toms. I had to agree that he was right; the names fitted them well. When it came to the two toms, the decision as to which should be which of the two remaining names was easy. One was a big grey-and-white brindle, my favourite of all the cats. He must, I told my grandfather, 'be Moscow'. And so it was.

When we told my mother what we were doing, she thought it ridiculous that a grown man, indeed an old man, should be 'filling a child's head with such nonsense'. I then reminded her that she had given me names for our two cows. That was different, she blustered. I was only a baby then. She then went on to say how ridiculous it was to be giving cats names and vowing that you'd never find her calling any cat by one of these 'fancy' names we'd given them. Imagine my surprise then, some weeks later, coming home from school to find her talking to someone in the kitchen. I could hear her voice as I came through the porch: 'Now, I think you're a good lad, Moscow.' She stopped talking when I came into the kitchen. There was no one else there. She was sitting in the inglenook with Moscow sitting beside her. I said nothing, and neither did she. Moscow just smiled his wonderfully enigmatic smile.

Shortly after that Fin had an accident. He chased some straying horses on the road near the house. One of them kicked him in the head. One eye was so badly damaged it had to be removed; the other eye was damaged also, but surgery and treatment retained about 60 per cent sight in it. He was aged about ten then, and the vet told us that the remaining eye would grow slowly weaker over the next year or so. It did, and two years later Fin was totally blind. For a day or two he tried to get around the barn-yard and the door-yard, stumbling here and there, bumping into things and whining piteously. My grandfather knew he must have him put down. Then something occurred which changed his mind.

I was working in a field beside the stream with grandfather, snagging turnips. We saw something moving along the headland near the stream. I got off my knees to get a better look. It was the big brindle cat, Moscow, walking ahead of the poor blind dog. Fin had his head held high, and the cat was waving his long tail to and fro under the dog's chin, leading him slowly along. My grandfather and I watched the pair's stately progress till they came right up to us; Moscow purring madly and smiling, as if to say, 'Look how good I am.' Poor Fin just stood there and whimpered softly, wagging his tail, a sad, crooked grin on his poor disfigured face. I had always believed that, like some people, some cats and dogs had beautiful smiles. Also, like some people, some cats and dogs never smiled. Fin smiled, but Butcher didn't; four of the six cats smiled. We were very lucky indeed … Moscow still had a beautiful smile.

That incident meant a reprieve for Fin. My grandfather put off the day when the dreaded decision to have him put down must be made. For the next few weeks, Moscow led the poor blind dog around the place, from kitchen to dooryard to haggard. They were inseparable. On one occasion they even appeared at the dancing platform, walking slowly, majestically across the dance floor, getting a big cheer and a round of applause.

Sadly, one morning shortly after that, Moscow disappeared. Fin sat in the porch, whimpering for his helper. But his helper never came. For two days the dog stumbled around, lost, confused, bumping against things. My grandfather and I spent many hours searching the fields for Moscow, knowing how he liked to hunt in the bog and along the cliff top. Eventually we found little taggles of his lovely, brindled coat strewn along the whin bushes. Very near the edge of the cliff we found a strip of his blood-stained skin lying in the grass. We knew then that our search was in vain. Poor old Moscow had ventured too near the foxes' run and had fallen victim to them. Next day we had Fin put down. We were all sad, particularly grandfather and myself. Two old smiling friends had left our life.

Fin was the first dog in my life. She had been in the household a few months before I was born. We grew up together. She was kind, faithful and totally trustworthy. She was very special to me and I cried a lot when she had to be put down. All my adult life I've had a dog in the household. When our last dog died my wife and I decided that at both 77 years of age, we were too old to look after a dog properly, to groom it and walk it. So for the first time we have no dog in the house. Imagine then my great surprise to find that one of my daughters got two dogs shortly after she had married and without ever having heard me mention my old friend Fin, she named one of her dogs … Fin! Full circle? Yes, I believe some things do come full circle.

23

From as far back as I can remember, I have always had a penchant for eavesdropping. It was as if I knew from a very early age that one day I would be a writer, and that these overheard conversations, these remembered impressions, would be the bricks and mortar of my future stories.

Toward the close of 1944, when the end of the war was imminent, my father took me to Dublin for the first time. I remember the exact date, Saturday 16 December, because on arrival in Dublin we heard that the famous band-leader Glen Miller was 'missing presumed lost'. It was the first time I'd ever been on a train. I had travelled by bus the previous September to boarding school, a mere 40 miles away, and was now on my first vacation. So this journey to Dublin seemed quite epic to me – over 100 miles, and by steam-driven train in a time when fuel was at a premium. My father explained to me how a steam engine worked. It had to have enough fuel in its bunker to keep up a head of steam all the way to its destination. At that time coal was rationed, the turf was usually very wet and timber was in short supply. The unfortunate fireman on a steam train in those war years had great difficulty just keeping the fire alight, never mind raising a head of steam.

So we chugged along through the dreary, wintry countryside. At every scheduled stop we took on board baskets and bags of supplementary fuel collected by the stationmaster and his family; their contribution to the war effort. This gave the dying fire a temporary fillip and carried us forward, chugging and hiccupping, to the next stop. Except once, on a slight gradient, when the engine came slowly to a halt. Driver, fireman and guard had to get down and scavenge along the hedges that bordered the line for whatever pieces of timber they could find to help revive the faltering fire and produce that all-important head of steam. They succeeded in getting us moving again, albeit slowly, and we reached Dublin over two hours later than the stated time of arrival.

We stayed with my father's sister in Blackrock and visited the National Gallery, the National Museum and several bookshops. We bought

Christmas presents in Clerys. Passing through Westmoreland Street, my father pointed out to me where he'd had his first job as a messenger boy with the famous pharmaceutical firm of Boileau and Boyd. He had worked there for over a year while waiting to get a place under his father, training to be a bothy-man, in the Phoenix Park.

On our way back to Kingsbridge Station, we visited a famous pub on the quays. My father explained that on his rare visits to Dublin, he always called to say hello to an old friend from Waterford who worked as a 'curate' in O'Meara's. It was afternoon and the place was quiet. While my father drank his pint and talked with his friend, I was parked on a high stool at the end of the counter and given a glass of Lemon Soda. There were few other customers. A countryman and his wife, laden with parcels, like ourselves going for the train. They were silent, each with a whiskey on the small table and a sad faraway look on their faces, so apart that each might have been waiting for someone else.

The only other customers were four men engaged in intense conversation. Two of them were pretty ordinary; the third was large and middle-aged. The fourth was younger than the others, a veritable giant, his great height and bulk accentuated by his wild, tousled hair and untrimmed beard. They all drank whiskey, with a bottle placed in the centre of the table from which they replenished their glasses as quickly as they emptied them. They were what my father always referred to as 'serious drinkers'. They were talking about someone named Brownie, who was related to the giant with the tousled hair. Brownie had died recently and the big fellow was inconsolable. He told the other men he hadn't slept for nearly a week now. And I saw this big, strong man cry right there at the table. I knew what they were saying, but I didn't have the vocabulary to describe it then, as I now do.

Just then my father called me: we were leaving. On the way to the station I asked him about the men at the table. The barman had told him that 'the big fella' was an English writer, and the others were friends of his from *The Irish Times* newspaper. The writer was known to be a conscientious objector to the war and was staying in County Meath. I had to ask what a 'conscious objector' was. I also asked what the writer's name was, on the off-chance that he was someone whose name I would know from my days at national school. My father thought the barman had said his name was White and he wrote about King Arthur. Was it T. H. White, I asked. It was, indeed, my father said. I think I then surprised him by saying, very excitedly, that I knew him from his books about King Arthur, which the Master had read for us at national school, and loaned to me to read myself.

Later, sitting in the old steam train bumping our long, slow way home I kept thinking of the great opportunity I had lost. I could have talked to White and told him how much I loved his books. I also kept wondering who was his close friend, Brownie, who had died. I read many of White's books after that, but it was not until 1959 when I worked in Dublin with *The Irish Press* newspaper that I read *The Godstone and The Black-ymor* and realised that Brownie had been a dog. A dog very dear to the old bachelor writer. As a young man White had decided that it was much more satisfactory to give his affection to animals – dogs and falcons – than to humans. He wrote then, 'animals never let you down, humans invariably do.'

That was part of the Brownie mystery solved

after so many, many years. I had to wait until much later, 1967 to be exact, to discover the circumstances of Brownie's death. Reading Sylvia Townsend Warner's wonderful biography of White, I found that Brownie had died rather suddenly while White was in Dublin one day. He had left her in the care of the farming family with whom he boarded in County Meath.

That wartime trip to Dublin was my first foray into the big, outside world and my grandfather was eager to hear my story of it. The day after we came home, he and I went for one of our strolls across the fields. The older I got, the more I loved those strolls with my grandfather. On this occasion he began to talk about how I had now started to 'go out into the world'. I was at boarding school meeting other boys from all over the country. I had just been to Dublin with my father, and I had previously been to Waterford with poor old Luke. So, he said, very seriously, there was something he must tell me. Now was the time – the right time. He was a great believer in the time being right for everything, often quoting some lovely lines about there being 'a season for everything under heaven'.

He then explained to me that there were certain things that only showed up in families every second generation. The 'gift' he was about to talk about had been his from birth; then it had skipped my uncles' (his sons) generation and was now showing itself in my generation, in me. He was sure, after much thought and listening to 'the voice inside him', that I had this gift and needed now to be told about it. Grandfather was also a great believer in listening to 'the voice inside him' and trusted it implicitly. Just then we were crossing one of the little meadow fields, where the two cows grazed every day. We came upon a cow dung. He asked me what it was. Naturally I said, 'a cow dung'. He asked me to try again. I said, rather hesitantly, 'a cowpat'. He stopped walking, shook his head and explained that they were 'polite' terms used to describe the objects scattered about the field. In 'real' language it was, he said, a cow shit.

There was silence between us for a little while. Then he told me of this great gift with which I had been born. I had the same gift as himself, the gift of a built-in 'shit detector'. Not the kind that detected cow shit, but the kind that detected the shit that people talked in life, the shit way people lived their lives. That's what it was for. And now that I knew I had it, I must use it. Learn to detect the thing from as far off as possible and cry out against it. I asked him then what should I cry out when I had detected it. He stopped walking again. I could use his 'war-cry' he said. In the face of all who used this hateful blather, I could cry out, 'Shit maru!' He laughed as he said that, adding that that would make them think. But, he concluded, when you learned to detect the 'shit maru' at a good distance, you should then do the only wise thing and stay as far away as possible from it.

As with all the advice my grandfather ever gave me, I took it and acted on it, though initially I may have doubted its validity. However, I found it to be the best gift I've ever been given, the gift of that shit-detector. It has worked for me all my life. I used to worry a little as I got older if the wonderful instrument within me would lose its sharpness with the passing years – get blunted and less sensitive. However, the converse has been true. My shit-detector has become sharper and more sensitive as the years have passed.

Over a quarter of a century ago, I could detect the abomination a mile off; now, incredibly, I can detect it two miles off. I often think that in his dying, grandfather may have passed on some of the potency of his gift to me.

24

I only wish I could say I was happy at my new school, but I can never. The Christian Brothers there were a very unhappy lot. And they visited their unhappiness on the pupils.

By the time I was twelve and had spent two years at boarding school, I knew that formal education would never have any place in my life. Indeed, I knew after six months but remained there out of a feeling of loyalty to my old friend and mentor, Luke Tarpey. Then I remembered what the letter from Luke's solicitor had said about my deciding that formal education was not for me. I suddenly realised that he must have suspected I would not want to go on. So at the end of that second year I left boarding school without any feeling of having let Luke down, but with a definite feeling of having disappointed my parents, particularly my mother. I know she had hopes that I might go on and become a doctor or a lawyer.

These hopes of my mother were never verbalised, but I could feel her hurt and wished I could do something to assuage it. But what could I do if I was to remain true to myself? That was my first, very painful lesson in how impossible it is sometimes to do what you think is right for you and avoid hurting someone you love. For a while I thought I would compromise and give formal education another chance. I would accede to whatever my mother had planned for me.

She arranged for me to go to school at the Christian Brothers in Tramore town and board from Monday to Friday with her married sister in that town. Her sister's husband owned a bakery and they had six children. The eldest, David, was just my age. I was very happy in that household, helping out in the bakery after school and becoming very much a part of the family. My cousins and I became close friends for that year, but afterwards, as so often happens, our lives took us in different directions and we seldom saw each other again.

I only wish I could say I was happy with my new school, but I can never. The Christian Brothers there were a very unhappy lot, and they visited their unhappiness on the pupils. The infamous black leather strap was in constant use. One brother, who shall be known here as

Brother X, had a wonderfully sadistic way of handling any difficult boy. He would grab the boy by the lobe of the ear and slowly lift him off the ground. He would then 'jog' the helpless victim up and down a few times until the soft flesh at the bottom of the ear would tear and the boy shrieked in pain. Incredibly, the boy would then be told to go to the Brothers' House and have the housekeeper put a plaster on the torn flesh which, by then, would have begun to bleed. Such solicitude from the person who had deliberately inflicted the injury was inexplicable. In that first short term before Christmas this must have taken place eight or nine times in class. All of us in that class waited for something to happen, and something did happen …

One afternoon when we were all very quiet after a particularly heavy session of using the black leather strap on several boys, the door of the classroom was kicked open, shattering the two glass panels. A large man loomed in the open doorway, over six feet tall, dressed in a workman's overalls. Looking around he walked slowly, menacingly, across to where Brother X stood.

'Are you Brother X?' the big man bellowed.

'I am. What can I do for you, sir?'

'Nothing,' the big man shouted, reaching out and grabbing both of the Brother's ears, jogging him up and down, up and down, until we began to fear the ears must come off in his hands. Then he set Brother X down and delivered such a punch to the chin that our teacher went flying across the floor, crashing into a big bookcase and displacing dozens of books.

'That is for ALL the boys whose ears you ever damaged,' the big man thundered and then walked away.

By then, other teachers had come in and were taking Brother X away. We all sat at our desks, transfixed by this display of rough justice. Looking back on the incident now, I think we all felt like cheering at watching Brother X being humiliated, but we could only sit there in silence and feel in some strange way humiliated ourselves by such violence. This was an early and salutary lesson: violence always begets violence and starts a chain that is very difficult to break. We never saw Brother X again.

After that episode my mind was made up. I'd had enough of formal education. But I had to let my poor mother down as gently as I could. So I devised a plan that would show her I had it in me to learn but also, when I chose, not to learn. I studied very hard for the remainder of that year. In the end-of-year exams I took seven subjects and achieved seven honours. Everyone was thrilled – my teachers and, most important of all, my mother. I stayed on for another year and deliberately did not study at all. I took eight subjects in my end-of-year exams and managed to fail them all. After that, the school didn't want me and I didn't want the school. My father and mother accepted that I could learn when I wanted to, but I just didn't want to learn a whole lot of subjects in which I had not the slightest interest. I was not quite fourteen. There were things I could help out with at home, while they used whatever few contacts they had to find me a job. They accepted that I needed some time to find what I really wanted to do in life. Until then they would do everything they could to help.

There is a sad little sequel to the story of Brother X. Twenty-five years after the punch-up in the classroom, I was making a radio documentary for RTÉ and needed some material from an Irish Christian Brothers' archive. The archive was located in one of their monasteries in the Irish midlands. I went there one warm afternoon in

May to select my material. They had told me on the phone that the archive office was located in a building separate from the main building. After I had parked my car, I saw an old Brother hoeing some flower beds nearby, I went over to ask him for directions. He turned round as I approached. After all the years, I recognised Brother X instantly. I showed no sign of this recognition but asked him where the archive building was. As he told me, I studied him: the same saturnine face, same yellowing skin, same rheumy eyes. But the eyes sunken now with the stare some old people get when the life-force, like the butt-end of a candle, is slowly guttering out. He wore a black soutane, the front stained with marks of food. I was tempted to make myself known to him but didn't. Instead, I just thanked him and said, 'Retired?'

'Oh, yes,' he said, 'a long time now.'

So I left him to his hoeing and his demons; an old sad man with a food-stained soutane and the piteous cries of boys with torn ear lobes twisting all day in his tormented memory. And by night those same cries, more strident now, echoing along the periphery of his tortured dreams.

25

The mountains all round us were so blue and quiet that I couldn't help wondering, as I looked up at the great blue wall, what might be on the other side.

I had a great wish to go to see the Comeragh mountains. For months my grandfather had been telling me of Crotty the Robber and how we should go and see his lake and the crags where he lived. So on a fine summer morning we left early in the donkey-trap, pulled by my old friend Paycock. The Gusher came with us. Paycock was slow, and it took us nearly half the day to get there. Afterwards The Gusher put it very well when he said that it took half a day to get there and half a day to come back; the other half we spent on the mountain.

After the two hills at the head of our Glen, which we always referred to as 'the mountains', the Comeraghs looked enormous; dark blue in the summer mist from the distance, but as we got closer, a lighter blue, with deep-cut crevasses. By arrangement we met a 'mountain man' at Mahon Bridge who my grandfather knew. We untackled Paycock and left him to his well-earned rest. We then set off up through the foothills in a cart pulled by a sturdy horse. After a very bumpy ride the horse and cart could go no further, and neither could my grandfather and The Gusher. So we left them to enjoy their packed lunch and a few bottles of porter, seated contentedly in the deep heather. I continued the steep climb with the mountain man. After what seemed an eternity we reached Crotty's Lake. Here we sat down to eat our lunch of home-made brown bread and bottles of milk.

While we ate, my guide pointed out Crotty's famous rock, from which the famous highway-man commanded a view of the countryside for fifteen miles and could see all the movements of the militia. However, a detail from that same militia eventually captured Crotty and took him to Waterford Gaol where he was executed and his head displayed on a spike outside the gate. His wife and child were hunted down in the Comeraghs and thrown to their death from one of the high crags. There was great mourning among the poor people of the district on hearing of Crotty's death. For several years he had been a Robin Hood figure to them, giving them the money he stole from the wealthy.

I remember so clearly lying in the heather, absolutely terrified by the tales the mountain man was telling me, trying to remind myself that it had all happened over 200 years before. The mountains all round us were so blue and quiet that I could not help wondering as I looked up at the great blue wall what might be at the other side. I asked my guide. He said there was only one thing of great interest on the other side and that was the famous Abbey of Mount Melleray, about ten miles away. I told him I had read a lot about Mount Melleray and he was very interested. Beyond knowing that the monastery was famous and of great interest, he didn't seem to know anything about it.

As we were making our slow journey home later, I thought a lot about Mount Melleray and of all I had read about it. I had no idea it was just the other side of the Comeraghs. Though I could not know then of Graham Greene's words about letting the future in, I could feel some strong intimation of that door beginning to open. Looking back as Paycock trotted along, I could see the Comeraghs slowly turning to a dark blue as evening came down and the sky paled to a milky white. Beyond that pale sky and that dark mountain, I was becoming aware of the existence of a whole new world, a whole new life. The Gusher commented on how quiet I was, and my grandfather, winking at me, just said, 'He's thinking!' And I am sure, at that very moment, the old man knew exactly what I was thinking, so close were we in spirit and had been from the cradle.

26

*Standing in the well of the boat,
wallowing and rolling in the huge
Atlantic swell sweeping up the
estuary, the black-and-white striped
lighthouse was the most gigantic solid
building I had ever seen. To the south
east, two small coasters ploughed their
way westward. They looked like toy boats
bobbing about in the great moving maw of
the blue and white water.*

For the week after that visit to the Comeraghs, I moved around at home as if in a trance. I kept thinking of the great blue wall of the mountains and what was on the other side. Mount Melleray Abbey! I had read a book about it when I was eleven, a book given me by Fr Jim. I now searched for the book and read it again. That was a different world, no doubt. I longed to go and see it for myself. How to get there was the problem. It was only twenty miles from our house. That, I thought, was a distance I could easily cycle. But I would have to bring someone with me. I talked to my younger brother Michael and gave him the book about Melleray. He was not as interested in the place as I was, but he said he would go with me. It would, he felt, be a great adventure, and we could stop and have a good rest at half-way. After a couple of days of talking about this adventure, we talked to my father about it.

Father liked the idea and said he would look over our bicycles and make sure they were road-worthy. That very evening, after the Rosary, we talked to my grandfather and mother about it. My grandfather was really excited, but my mother was fearful of two very young boys cy-cling twenty miles there and twenty miles back. However, after a few days of talking to her, she came round to giving the trip her blessing. I then spoke to Fr Jim about it, and he wrote a letter to the Guestmaster, advising him that two boys from his parish wished to come and stay for a week at the Guest House. He gave the date of our arrival and the approximate time. He got a reply within a few days from the Guestmaster, Fr Virgilius, saying we would be very welcome.

We were overjoyed. That weekend my father and mother went to Tramore and bought us a handsome pair of pannier bags to hold whatever we were going to carry. It was August and the weather was warm and dry so we could travel light. Mother also bought us a large Thermos flask, to take some tea for when we broke our journey. It was the first time I had seen a Thermos and I was fascinated at how the tea would stay hot for so long. Grandfather, as excited about the journey as we were, gave us each a pound note with which to buy lemonade along the way.

As we were not due to depart for another two weeks, my grandfather thought it would be nice for us to go to the lighthouse at Hook Head, on the Wexford coast. He knew one of the keepers there and could arrange a visit. He told me later that he was very decided that I should not settle into just working about the little place and let time drift by. He was decided that I should see as many places outside The Glen as possible, prepare myself for 'going out into the world'. And then, he added with a great laugh, that is where I'd need my 'shit detector', out there where most people were full of 'it' and not to be trusted. As a child, I always thought that my grandfather felt you could only trust about one in every hundred people. Since I have grown to manhood, I have found that to be way off the mark. You can only trust one in every two hundred people, if you're lucky.

We made the crossing to Hook Head from Dunmore East by fishing boat. Standing in the well of the boat, rolling in the huge Atlantic swell sweeping up the estuary, the black-and-white striped lighthouse tower was the most gigantic solid building I had ever seen. As we wallowed in the trough of the big seas, it towered above us on its bare promontory, dominating landscape and seascape. Seaward, to the south east, two small coasters ploughed their way westward, their decks awash. They looked like toy boats, bobbing about in the great moving maw of the blue and white water.

As we got nearer we could see the keepers' houses behind the compound wall. They looked like toy houses in the giant shadow of the great tower. In those days some of the keepers had families living at the lighthouse, and I spent most of the day playing with the bigger children, learning a lot about how the lighthouse worked. Three of the boys, who were about my own age, were just longing to be eighteen, old enough to go and train to be lighthouse keepers. In the afternoon, my grandfather's friend took us right up to the top of the tower. With him I climbed the many steps, losing count after fifty-something. My grandfather couldn't make the climb due to his disabled leg.

As we climbed the keeper explained how the new lighthouse tower had been built round the old tower. The old tower had been a monastery and he showed me the monks' cells – tiny cramped places set into the old walls. There was also a lovely vaulted ceiling of what had been their chapel in the centre of the tower. At every level of that tortuous climb to the top, there were long narrow windows framing views of the tumbling sea, the cloudless sky and the green, undulating, bucolic summer countryside.

When we reached the top of the tower, my head was spinning. Spinning from the climb and spinning from the tales the keeper was telling me – of how this was the oldest lighthouse in the

British Isles, going back to the fifth century when a Welsh monk and hermit, St Dubhan, had established the first primitive beacon here. Poor Dubhan, the keeper said, became so tired of removing the dead bodies of shipwrecked sailors from the rocks that he decided to set up some kind of warning fire for ships approaching the estuary.

Ever since that first long-ago visit to Hook Head, I have been in love with lighthouses. In love with the lonely places where they are set. In love with the Spartan, though comfortable, conditions. In love with the cleanliness of the great towers themselves. In love with their shining brasswork and their polished lanterns. But in love, most of all, with the great lights endlessly raking the sea and sky night after night, warning ships of the perils of jagged rocks and white water. And full of admiration for the men, and occasionally women, who ensure that the lights never fail to be lit and kept burning.

We left at dusk to come back to Dunmore East. As the boat rounded the head the light was switched on above us in the great tower. It was wonderful to be that close to it and watch it sweep way out across the roiling waters of the estuary. Though I did not know it then, this was to be a perfect preparation for what awaited us at Mount Melleray.

Two weeks later, on what the poet Patrick Kavanagh called 'an apple-ripe September morning', Michael and I set out for Mount Melleray. The sky was cloudless, and my grandfather, a renowned judge of weather, said it would be a very hot day. We set out at seven in the morning to get some of the journey over before the big heat. Within the first half-hour on the road we had passed all the places we knew. From then on it was 'discovering' places that had just been names on the map – Dunabrattin, Boatstrand, Bonmahon, Stradbally, Clonea Strand. We decided that, as we were making great time, we would stop and rest for half an hour at Clonea Strand. Saving our flask of tea for later we bought lemonade and biscuits, sat on a grassy mound and looked out at the bright blue sea. Already we were beginning to feel like real travellers.

Just past the end of the Comeragh Mountains, we stopped again to see the monument to the famous greyhound Master McGrath. Bred nearby, this wonder dog had won the famous

Waterloo Cup three times, and we had heard 'The Ballad of Master McGrath' sung very often at the Open Night at home. We laughed and said we'd be able to tell the next Open Night that we had seen the famous monument. A little further on the land becomes quite flat and cycling was much easier. The great heat had brought with it a light haze, so we could not yet see the Knockmealdown Mountains where the Abbey of Mount Melleray stood. After journeying on in the great heat for several miles, we stopped where the edge of a huge forest came down to touch the roadside fence. We could hear the music of a little stream flowing out of the forest under the roadside bridge and on into the flat meadowland. It reminded us of home, and for a moment, though we did not admit it to each other then, we felt very far from home and vaguely lost. Also we felt very hot and hungry, so we took off our shoes and socks and waded into the stream. I thought of Mary Rose but kept that thought to myself. We then drank our flask of tea and ate the home-made brown bread and home-cured bacon.

Then we pushed on. We were tiring greatly now and the last eight miles seemed like twenty.

As with Dungarvan, we bypassed Cappoquin. From now on the road led up out of the flat country and we could see the Knockmealdown Mountains but no sign of the monastery. The road dipped a little and we came round a sharp bend. There set into the brown mountainside, the lovely granite stone glistening almost white in the sunlight, stood the magnificent abbey church. I have been back to Mount Melleray many times over the years, and the suddenness of that view never ceases to surprise and delight me.

27

From the time we returned home from Mount Melleray, I could feel a tide turning in my young life. That door to the future that Graham Greene wrote about had, without my knowing it then, opened for me, and there was no going back. The inexorable tide of life was already bearing me away from The Glen, as it had borne Mary Rose before me.

From that first visit to Mount Melleray, I have been in love with the Cistercian way of life, in love with the place itself. The place is so at one with the lives being lived out there. The great granite church on the bleak inhospitable mountainside, from which unpromising terrain the tireless toil of the monks over many years has produced wide acres of fertile land. Then there is the absence of any kind of extraneous decoration in the church or in the cloister. The crucifixes found in various locations are made of carved oak. The chalice used at Mass is made of carved stone. Even the icons that adorn many such churches are absent here. Here, simplicity is everything.

The monks are humble men, simple men, though in many cases erudite and highly educated men, many of them ex-medical doctors, ex-lawyers, ex-accountants, ex-teachers. That black and white habit, the voluminous white cloak, the rough leather boots make them all look exactly alike. They all have that kind, helpful demeanour, which I am sure Fr Jim's 'Humble Nazarene' possessed. To talk with them, to walk with them, to work with them is to feel so much closer to Jesus. Even as boys of fourteen and twelve and a half, Michael and I could sense we were in a different world.

When we arrived, saddle sore and weary from the journey, we were met by the Guest Master, Fr Virgilius, a small, rotund, balding monk in his mid-thirties. He was so welcoming and jovial that it was hard to believe we were in a Cistercian monastery, where we had imagined a great *gravitas* would prevail. Our bicycles were put safely away in a shed in the Guest House garden; indeed, so busy were we during the next two weeks, that we never even thought of using them until the day came to travel back home.

It is the rule in all Cistercian monasteries that there is no fee for boarding there. A discreet little notice in the Guest House parlour says that any donations guests wish to leave are very gratefully accepted to help defray the cost of running the Guest House. After tea that first evening, we explained to Fr Virgilius that we could not really afford to pay much but would gladly work in any way we could to help out. He was most kind and gracious and said we could help greatly by washing up after meals in the refectory, as there were sixteen guests. This we were glad to do. We explained that we were used to helping out on the little place at home and could help out with chores around the farm. This he thought was a fine idea, and he would talk to Brother Laurence, the farm manager, about it. In due course we were given 'light duties' around the farmyard and the fields.

This we enjoyed immensely. The monks milked a herd of sixty cows every day, morning and evening. This was in the days before milking machines came to the monastery. We were not expected to do any of the actual milking; there was a small army of fourteen monks deployed at milking. From years of doing the job, they had become quick and expert at it. We were able to wash out milk churns and milking buckets and do various other light jobs about the dairy. We also helped out in the monastery bakery every morning when the newly baked bread came out of the big ovens. It was a very busy bakery. They baked every day for over sixty monks and whatever guests were in the Guest House. The Brother in charge of the bakery was very interested to know that our uncle had a bakery in Tramore and that I had worked there occasionally.

We also helped out in the butchery department, where the monks killed their own beasts – cattle, sheep and pigs. The monks themselves were not allowed, by the Rule, to eat meat with the exception of an ailing old monk who was advised by the doctor to do so. The meat was largely then for the Guest House table. The Brother in charge of the Butchery Department was fascinated when I told him of our grandfather's reputation for killing and curing. He loved, especially, how the old man 'cured' the pigs' heads on the pulley in our big, open chimney. The various departments must have communicated to Fr Virgilius our 'experience' of all these things. He joked with us and said what great monks we would make with all that expertise. We enjoyed all the work in the various departments, but we wished that the monks could talk to us. They were not, again by their strict Rule, allowed to talk to us or to each other but we communicated through smiles and gestures.

While all that work was wonderfully exciting, the most wonderful part of our stay for me was the chanting of the beautiful Plainchant by the monks in church many times a day. To hear the organ start and the voices of over sixty monks sing out the various Offices was then and still is for me the most moving experience. Michael usually stayed on in bed in the mornings until seven o'clock, but I got up when the great monastery bell rang out for the first Office of the day, called Vigils, at four o'clock. That, for me, was a magic time, when I would sit at the back of the choir in the semi-dark of morning and listen to the rhythmic rise and fall of the voices. And, afterward, when the monks had all left the choir, I would sit and watch the first of daylight flood the big stained-glass window and think of many things. Not least that I might someday become a monk myself.

After Vigils the Masses were celebrated at the little side-altars all round the church. That too was a magic time with the low-key voices of the priests as they celebrated Mass in the Latin rite. It was wonderful to hear the little bells tinkle at the Consecration, not all together, but at short intervals depending on how quickly or slowly each priest celebrated his Mass. This chorus of bells would ring out for five or six minutes. Then there was the odour of so many wax candles burning all together, two on each altar. And as each Mass ended then came the smell of the candles being snuffed out and the heady, sweet smell of the wicks and hot wax. The whole effect on me was quite hypnotic, and I would stagger in to the refectory for early breakfast with my mind a repository of peace and silence.

That was a dream I cherished for several years, but the great tide of life took me in other directions. Yet to this day I have remained a Cistercian at heart. I visited Mount Mellary countless times over the years and it has always been my spiritual home. I have written a lot about

Cistercian life. Indeed, one long article I wrote last year for a Catholic newspaper had to have a pseudonym rather than my own name. Without hesitation I signed it, *A Lay Cistercian*.

There have always been two places where I have regularly gone on 'pilgrimage' – the lighthouse and the Cistercian monastery. For me, they have a lot in common. The loneliness of the locations, the Spartan living conditions, the great unbroken silences and the ambience so conducive to bringing me face-to-face with myself; a place where there is no possibility of escaping that necessary confrontation.

Someone asked me recently where on earth I would most like to visit before I die. Without hesitation I answered Mount Melleray. I would love to see the place, listen to the Plainchant and talk with my old friend Fr Kevin, who at eighty-three is still working as Bursar there. We correspond regularly, and I tell him every spring of the trip I will make to see him. Both Fr Kevin and I know that, being crippled and in a wheelchair, I shall never make that journey. So, we must contend with what Henry Miller said when asked which was the greatest of all his great journeys. He said that 'the greatest journey in the world is the journey inward toward the self'. So I, from my little house overlooking Dublin Bay and the Baily Light, and Fr Kevin, from his monastery over a hundred miles away on the bare, brown Knockmealdown Mountains, must both set out on that journey inward, in the certain faith that we shall meet somewhere along the way.

From the time Michael and I returned home from Mount Melleray, I could feel a tide turning in my young life. That door to the future that Graham Greene wrote about had, without my knowing it then, opened for me and there was no going back. That inexorable tide of life was bearing me away from The Glen, as it had borne Mary Rose before me. But I was resolved that I would always remember that special place where I had grown up, and the special people who had loved and moulded me. And I also resolved that I would someday write about it with integrity and love. I hope that I have.